COL

How to Get a Management NVQ, Level 3

Book 1: Mandatory Units

In Memory of

Stanley Billington (1950–1982)

How to Get a Management NVQ, Level 3

Book 1: Mandatory Units

Richard Johnson and Cathy Parker

Letts Educational
Aldine Place
LONDON
W12 8AW
Tel: 0181-740 2268
Fax: 0181-743 8451
e-mail: he@lettsed.co.uk

Acknowledgements

We would like to begin by acknowledging all those candidates who have helped develop the concept for this book, as it was their need for a supporting text that was the driving force behind its development. In addition, the content of the book has evolved through supporting candidates through various stages of their qualification. We are indebted to those people who have allowed us to refine our methods and advice over the past four years. Special thanks should go to Heather Muir and Alan Follett for their support, ideas and discussion, and to Donna for her typing skills. We are sure that we will continue to learn from the experiences and efforts of others, and would therefore encourage readers of our book to contact us (FreshThink@aol.com) with their comments and feedback.

A CIP catalogue record for this book can be obtained from the British Library
ISBN 1-85805-345-5

Copyright Richard Johnson and Cathy Parker © 1998

The National Occupational Standards for Management were developed by the MCI with DfEE funding. This material is Crown copyright and is reproduced under licence from the Controller of Her Majesty's Stationery Office.

Designed and typeset by Ian Foulis & Associates, Plymouth, Devon

Printed and bound in Great Britain by Ashford Colour Press, Gosport, Hants

Contents

Preface

How to Get a Management NVQ (Level 3) has been developed as a direct result of our involvement in supervisory development programmes across a number of industries and sectors, from social services to mining and everything in between.

Challenged with the task of supporting managers and supervisors in their quest to achieve their NVQ, a major issue confronted us: the realities of work-based learning. What were NVQ candidates to do when they could not get access to advice? Our research suggests that although the majority of managers and supervisors collect the evidence for their NVQ at work, the amount of peace and tranquillity they need in order to reflect and write up their analysis is unlikely to be found in a busy office, with 101 things still on the 'to do' list. Calmer surroundings are usually found at home, often after the children/partner/dog/cat have settled for the evening, at which time so too has the manager's NVQ advisor. So the need for supportive materials became apparent. Managers live and work in the oddest of places – they cannot always get to centralised seminars, workshops and classes held at their local college, TEC or training centre. *How to Get a Management NVQ* seeks to address these issues – to give you your own portable advisor that never sleeps and that aims to support you during the process of obtaining your NVQ.

To get your Management NVQ you will need to identify, analyse and reference hard evidence of your competence as a manager; *How to Get a Management NVQ* simply assists you in this process. Unit by unit, chapters help you to interpret the standards required by the qualification and make them meaningful and relevant to *your* job in *your* workplace. Each page has an area set aside for note making, evidence identification and even labelling for future reference. Relevant questions are asked, suggestions for areas of reflection and analysis are made, and recommendations for items of hard evidence are also included.

Anyone alarmed by the amount of jargon associated with NVQs will be pleased to learn that the book is written in plain English. NVQ jargon is explained and the portfolio-building process examined and illustrated. *How to Get a Management NVQ* will confirm and reassure your thoughts and reflections, supporting your ideas and actions. It will also drive you towards identifying new areas of work and evidence for inclusion in your NVQ. In contrast to alternative, generic texts, this series gets to the heart of the practical aspects of undertaking a Management NVQ and will assist you to achieve the qualification without compromising your approach. Enjoy the process!

Richard Johnson and Cathy Parker

Introduction

'To realise our ambition, we must all develop and sustain a regard for learning at whatever age. For many people this will mean overcoming past experiences which have put them off learning. For others it will mean taking the opportunity, perhaps for the first time, to recognise their own talent, to discover new ways of learning and to see new opportunities opening up.'

David Blunkett, Secretary of State for Education and Employment,
'The Learning Age', 1988

Background

This book has been conceived and published during an exciting time for learning and development. The new Labour government has announced its commitment to 'lifelong learning', major companies refer to themselves as 'learning organisations', and academics and practitioners in the field announce the arrival of 'the learning century' (Longworth and Davies, 1996). Obviously, those responsible for the nation's education and training appear to have welcomed these ideas. But what do all these concepts and labels mean to *learners* themselves? In terms of alterations to 'the learning system', the outcomes of change are apparent. New forms of qualification, such as NVQs, are rivalling traditional ones, and new ways of learning, far different to the ones most of us grew up with, are being championed. NVQs are vocational qualifications that rely on a myriad of approaches to learning and development, designed to meet the needs of industry and the individual rather than those of the educational providers. In a review of 100 NVQs and SVQs carried out by Gordon Beaumont (1997), the benefits of adopting NVQs were seen to outweigh the costs by 77 per cent of users. Nevertheless, despite the interest in and commitment to the concepts of lifelong learning and the integration of the term 'NVQ' into our everyday vocabulary, much confusion surrounds these topics.

Who is this book for?

This book has been written to support any candidate (or potential candidate) working with the revised MCI management standards at Level 3 (which were launched in January 1998). The book focuses on the five *mandatory* units of the qualification. As NVQs are a relatively new form of qualification, many candidates feel in the dark when it comes to actually doing one. Those in search of help and support cannot always access it, for a variety of reasons. Because of the demand for the qualification, many organisations and individuals have found themselves in the role of provider, sometimes with little experience or training. Another issue is the nature of the qualification itself. It is a work-based qualification to be completed, primarily, in the workplace. This means that those studying for it cannot rely on traditional means of support (weekly classes, fellow students, etc.).

What does it do?

As a result of being involved with Management NVQs over the past five years, we have realised that although every portfolio put forward for assessment is different, the process each candidate goes through, the problems they face and the questions they ask, are all very similar. It is these issues that we address in this book. By working through its contents, you will understand the requirements of the mandatory units of the qualification and avoid replicating some of the mistakes of those who have gone through the process before you. No book can or should replace a good advisor, but by using both sources of support you can ensure that you make the best possible use of your time with her or him.

Structure

The book is divided into two parts. The first part of the book explains the background to and nature of the qualification so that you can understand why you are studying for it. This section looks at the practicalities of progressing your NVQ by explaining the process of portfolio building and also introduces the other people who will be important to you as you progress your NVQ – people such as your advisor and assessor. Most importantly, this section also tells you about the level of service you can reasonably expect from these people, information that we hope will help to raise the standard and recognition of the qualification to the level it deserves. The second part of the book concentrates on actually *doing* your NVQ. By working through each chapter, using the prompts provided, you will soon find that you have a portfolio of evidence ready for assessment. We have also included the experiences of two real-life candidates so that you can see that you are not alone in your experiences.

Part One   An Introduction to Management NVQs

The first part of this book explains Management NVQs. It will explain what one is, the background to the qualification, the people involved, and how to build a portfolio of evidence. You may need to refer to the glossary (page 205) to get the most out of this section. If you are new to the NVQ process we recommend that you read this section fully. If you are familiar with this type of qualification, you may still find that it contains some useful information.

CHAPTER 1

What is a Management NVQ?

The first question any candidate asks is: 'What is a Management NVQ?' This chapter, therefore, aims to answer this question. We do this first by establishing the background to Management NVQs. This will enable you to understand the growth of the NVQ movement. Next we define and explain the nature of the qualification itself, so that you understand exactly what you are striving to achieve. We compare the award to other, more traditional qualifications to help you understand the level of the qualification for which you are studying. Finally, we summarise the process of achieving the qualification, so that you have a realistic idea of the amount of time and work involved in achieving your Management NVQ at Level 3.

Background

Vocational education and training in management has received central government support from its inception. Two government reports – *The Making of British Managers* (Constable and McCormick, 1987) and *The Making of Managers* (Handy, Gow and Moloney, 1987) – identified the need for competence-based education and training. This need coincided with the establishment of the National Council for Vocational Qualifications (NCVQ) and the Scottish Qualifications Authority (SQA) in 1980. NCVQ is now the Qualifications and Curriculum Authority (QCA) and it oversees all 896[1] NVQs, including all six Management NVQs.

The Management NVQs were developed by the Management Charter Initiative (MCI) and were first introduced in 1991. The MCI was set up to form a link between government, industry and education in order to develop the Management NVQs and to foster and sustain long-term commitment to their success. This commitment has continued to the present, with the Labour government signalling its intention to support the continued adoption of NVQs across all industries. Over 1,600,000 NVQs have now been awarded.

As an NVQ candidate, you are certainly not alone, but what accounts for this level of interest in Management NVQ programmes? It can be traced back to two economic reports of the 1980s, commissioned by the government. Both the Handy Report (Confederation of British Industry) and the McCormick Report (National Economic Development Office) supported the NVQ movement through their examination of management development and education in the UK.

---

[1] This figure represents all NVQs at all levels (compiled from *DataNews*, Winter 1997/98).

Their conclusions were as follows:

- ■ Management training is a key factor in economic growth.

- ■ UK managers receive little or no training.

- ■ Existing management training provision was too small for such a vast labour pool.

- ■ Existing provision was too eclectic; formats need to be standardised and nationally recognised across industries.

- ■ Any new framework should emphasise on-the-job training and personal development.

Of course, the success of NVQs is not wholly dependent on the support of government. To become a viable alternative to other forms of management development, NVQs needed to appeal to employers. NVQs represent an economic alternative to traditional training methods because the costs incurred in terms of staff replacement and related expenses are considerably lower than those associated with traditional qualifications. This is because development occurs on the job and is directly relevant to the manager's performance. This can be compared to classroom-based methods of training, which are often not directly relevant to the manager's job and take place outside the workplace.

Finally, there are the candidates themselves. The qualification has to be relevant to their needs, as they are the ones who actually have to make the effort to get it. Because of the changing nature of work, employees find themselves under increasing pressure. A number of factors contribute to this; for instance, downsizing means that, in many organisations, there are fewer employees left to do the same (or sometimes more) work. This puts pressure on those who want to attend day-release courses to obtain a qualification. Because of the harsh economic conditions facing many organisations, funding for this type of development has often been severely reduced. Anecdotal evidence from candidates also suggests that managers (especially those with families) are increasingly reluctant to give up evenings and weekends to attend courses. Nevertheless, because of growing uncertainty among many in employment (fuelled by the rising number of temporary contracts, endless calls for early retirement, rounds of redundancies, etc.), managers need qualifications that reflect their skills and experience. It is hardly surprising that a qualification as flexible as an NVQ, which can be undertaken at times convenient for the candidate, is proving so popular among employees concerned about the content of their curriculum vitae.

Definition of NVQs

A National Vocational Qualification is defined as

> 'a statement of competence relevant to employment. It is this statement which specifies the competence to be achieved. It is the basis from which assessment procedures and recording and certification can be derived'

QCA, 1988

The key part of this definition is the issue of competence. The Training Agency (1989) has defined competence as the ability to:

▪ Perform whole work roles (perform – not just know about – the whole job rather than just specific skills and tasks).

▪ Perform to the standards expected in employment (not just 'training' standards or standards divorced from industrial reality).

▪ Perform in real working environments (with all the associated pressures and variations of real work).

An NVQ prescribes standards of competence that you have to meet and consolidates these standards into a formal qualification. NVQs are based on explicit standards of competence, which are written down for everybody to see, in a standardised and nationally recognised format. NVQ statements of competence are identified from an analysis not of educational and training programmes, but of employment requirements. The analysis is carried out by, or on behalf of, employers and employees in the relevant sector, and the final product (i.e. the NVQ) has to be endorsed by them and approved by the Qualifications and Curriculum Authority (QCA) before it can be offered to candidates. The Management Charter Initiative (MCI) carried out this function for the Management NVQs; they developed the standards and are therefore termed the lead body for the Management NVQs. This means that they are responsible for the upkeep of the standards. In the past, this has meant rewriting them to ensure that they continue to be relevant to the needs of industry. By having nationally agreed standards of competence laid down for managers, any manager who can demonstrate that she or he meets these standards is, by definition, competent. For the first time, competent managers have an opportunity to prove it.

Content

All NVQs can be broken down into a number of constituent parts (Figure 1):

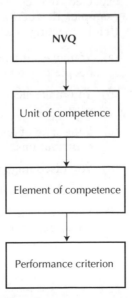

Figure 1
An illustration of the constituent parts of all NVQs

Units of competence

Units of competence refer to key aspects of management. For example, there are five mandatory units in the Management NVQ at Level 3. These are:

- Unit A1 – Maintain activities to meet requirements
- Unit B1 – Support the efficient use of resources
- Unit C1 – Manage yourself
- Unit C4 – Create effective working relationships
- Unit D1 – Manage information for action

As you can see, a unit neatly encapsulates an area of management, for instance Unit D1 is concerned with the information and decision-making side of management. In addition to these five units, you have to pick two optional units from a choice of eight. It is important that the optional units you pick reflect the job you do, otherwise you will not be able to generate or collect suitable evidence. Before you decide on your choice of optional units, you should talk to your advisor.

Elements of competence

Within each unit of competence there are elements of competence. These broadly reflect what managers are expected to do within each area (or unit) of management. Within Unit D1 ('Manage information for action'), the elements require you to prove that you:

- gather required information (Element D1.1);
- inform and advise others (Element D1.2);
- hold meetings (Element D1.3).

Performance criteria

Each element of competence is made up of a series of very specific performance criteria. These describe in detail what a manager is expected to achieve in order to demonstrate competence. For example, the performance criteria associated with Element D1.3 ('Hold meetings') are:

(a) You give sufficient notice of the meeting to allow the necessary people to attend.

(b) You make clear the purpose and objectives of the meeting at the start.

(c) Your style of leadership helps people to make useful contributions.

(d) You discourage unhelpful arguments and digressions.

(e) The meeting achieves its objectives within the allocated time.

(f) You give clear, accurate and concise information about the outcomes of the meeting promptly to those who need it.

Level

A Level 3 NVQ is for:

> 'practising managers or supervisors with: a tightly defined area of responsibility; some limited opportunity for taking decisions and managing budgets; responsibility for achieving specific results by using resources effectively; and responsibility for the allocation of work to team members, colleagues or contractors'

Management Charter Initiative (MCI), 1997

We have already established that competence-based qualifications focus on developing a candidate's work activities in line with nationally recognised standards. Because of this, competence-based qualifications differ considerably from academic qualifications, although comparisons between the two have been made. For example, a Level 3 MCI qualification in management (NVQ3) has been considered to be the equivalent of a National Diploma in a similar subject. Similarly, Level 4 MCI qualifications (NVQ4) have been equated with higher qualifications such as the Diploma in Management Studies (DMS). However, as competence-based qualifications have become more common in the workplace, it is apparent that comparisons of this kind are misleading and inaccurate since the nature and purpose of the two types of qualification are so different. In general, academic qualifications tend to focus on theoretical scenarios or the application of theory to a work situation. In contrast, competence-based qualifications focus on what candidates are already doing in their jobs and seek to develop their individual skills in the workplace.

Getting the award

In this section, we explain the process of obtaining a Management NVQ. Figure 2 represents the process as a diagram.

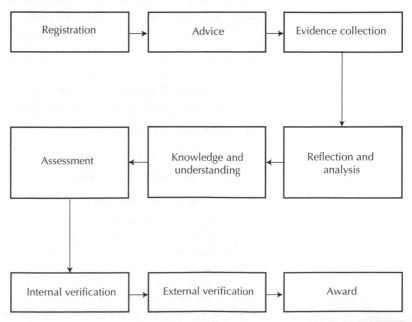

Figure 2
The process of obtaining an NVQ

Registration

The first stage of your NVQ will be registration with an awarding body. Currently, there are 16 organisations that are allowed to award a Management NVQ at Level 3; these are:

- City and Guilds
- Edexcel (formally BTEC)
- Engineering and Marine Training Authority
- Henley Management College
- Institute for Supervision and Management
- Institute of Personnel and Development
- London Chamber of Commerce and Ind. Examinations Board
- Management Verification Consortium
- RSA Examinations Board
- The College of Preceptors
- The Institute of Management
- The Institute of the Motor Industry
- The Institute of Operations Management
- The National Examining Board for Supervision and Management (NEBSM)
- The Open University
- University of Oxford Delegacy of Local Examinations

In terms of the management standards it makes no difference which awarding body you register with, since by their nature national standards do not change across providers. The only difference between awarding bodies is their interpretation of how certain aspects of the NVQ process should be managed. In this book we adopt a rigorous approach that will ensure you meet the requirements of the most demanding of awarding bodies.

You will register with your awarding body through an assessment centre. Assessment centres are organisations (or parts of organisations) that have been granted the opportunity to offer an awarding body's NVQ. In your case, your assessment centre could be:

- your own organisation;
- a local college/university;
- a private training provider;
- a professional body (e.g. The Institute of Management).

Often, two or more of these organisations work together to provide you with your NVQ. For example, within Durham County Council Social Services management candidates are registered with NEBSM (the awarding body) through East Durham Community College. However, the support services required by candidates (for example, advice and assessment) are provided by a combination of in-house staff and outside private training providers. Nevertheless, the responsibility for the standard of service all these people provide ultimately rests with the assessment centre. In the case of Durham County Council, this is now the responsibility of their Staff Development Section, which has recently been awarded assessment centre status from NEBSM (the awarding body).

From your perspective, one of the most important outcomes of registering is being given the management standards themselves. These are the standards of competence that you will have to demonstrate in order to be awarded your NVQ.

Advice

Once you have registered for your award, you should soon be allocated an advisor, who will help you achieve the requirements of the qualification. We detail what you can expect from your advisor in chapter 2. In this section we'll concentrate on where advice fits into the NVQ process. If you are one of a number of people studying for the same award, you may find that your early NVQ advice takes place within a workshop setting, where standard information can be more efficiently transmitted to a number of people. Typically, these workshops will cover much of the content we are focusing on in part one of this book. In other words, they serve as an introduction to the NVQ process. Some providers continue this workshop approach throughout the qualification. However, a good provider will offer these in addition to one-to-one advice.

The first one-to-one session, or *initial audit*, you are likely to have with your advisor will probably focus on understanding exactly what you do and what you have done in the past. The proper terminology for this is Accredited Prior Learning/Achievement (APL/A). In other words, your advisor will want to know if there is anything that you can put forward in order to save you unnecessary work. For example, if you already have a formal business qualification (such as an HNC in Business and Finance), it would be pointless to have to prove again your knowledge and understanding of the theoretical issues you have already covered in your HNC. In this case your qualification (the HNC) would be evidenced as Accredited Prior Learning. Of course, you would have to provide hard evidence of this. For example, you could include the certificate of award and the syllabus in your portfolio of evidence. You would also link this evidence back to the NVQ. For example, you could link the relevant syllabus items to specific requirements of the NVQ. As you progress your NVQ, your advisor will help you understand and interpret the standards, give you ideas for evidence, and often undertake mock assessments of your work before it is actually submitted for assessment.

Evidence collection

The idea behind the achievement of an NVQ is extraordinarily simple. A standard of competence is laid down (by the MCI) and you have to find some evidence to prove that you meet that standard. For example, one of the standards (performance criterion, to give it its proper name) requires you to '*assess your performance and identify your development needs at appropriate intervals*'. So, how could you prove that you actually do this in the workplace? One way might be to include documentation relating to any self-appraisal activities you carried out in the workplace. Or perhaps you discuss this type of thing with your manager or mentor during appraisal meetings. It will be up to you (with the help of your advisor) to decide what evidence will prove the requirements of the standard. A huge part of your NVQ will involve collecting evidence for your portfolio. We cover the types of evidence you can collect in more detail in chapter 3. As you get the hang of doing your NVQ, you will start to think more about evidence collection as part of your daily routine. For example, one candidate started to write more details about forthcoming meetings in her diary so that these diary pages could be photocopied and used as evidence. As a result, she found that she was more prepared for meetings as she now always knew what they were going to be about!

Reflection and analysis

Getting an NVQ is not merely a case of putting pieces of paper in a portfolio. Whatever evidence you submit in support of the management standards in which you are trying to prove competence *must* be explained. Your *reflection* upon and *analysis* of your evidence in relation to the management standards shows your assessor that you understand how you meet the requirements of the qualification. As assessors, we know how frustrating it is when candidates submit evidence in a portfolio with little or no attempt to explain *why* it is relevant. Remember, your assessor is there to help you, but she/he is not (always) telepathic! Reflection and analysis also gives you the opportunity to demonstrate your underlying knowledge and understanding of the related issues deemed important by the Management NVQ. You complete your reflection and analysis on stationery provided by your training provider/assessment centre. There is a completed example of this in Appendix 1.

Knowledge and understanding

An NVQ is not just about proving your competence through evidence gathered in the workplace. In addition to this, you need to prove that you understand *why* you do what you do. In other words, you will need to demonstrate that your actions at work are underpinned by your knowledge of relevant theories/principles/methods/models, etc. The way in which you meet the knowledge part of your NVQ may vary, depending on your provider. Some providers test knowledge through the use of formal tests and questions. Others prefer to set assignments that cover the requirements of the qualification. In some cases, knowledge and understanding may be linked to another course whose content meets some or all of the requirements of the NVQ. For example, you may have already studied for a business qualification and this achievement could be evidenced as Accredited Prior Learning (APL). A few providers (especially colleges and universities) have integrated NVQs into their existing academic provision. These providers are, in effect, offering a joint award: a certificate that credits the knowledge and under-standing of the candidate, and an NVQ that credits their competence in the workplace. Finally, your reflection and analysis can be used to demonstrate your underpinning knowledge and understanding. In our experience, it is advisable to make use of all these methods – choosing the most appropriate one for each situation as it arises.

Assessment

Assessment is the process whereby the evidence in your portfolio is compared with the NVQ standards in order to determine whether or not you are competent. This is a formal process and should not be confused with any general advice, feedback and support your assessor may give you during the development of your portfolio. When your portfolio is returned following assessment, you will find that the assessor has made a written copy of her/his assessment decision. There are three possible assessment decisions:

- Competent
- Not yet competent
- Insufficient evidence

If a candidate is not credited 'competent', the most likely assessment decision she or he will receive is that of insufficient evidence. In other words, a candidate may well be competent in an area of her or his job, but the evidence presented does not confirm this. Remember, your assessor is often external to your organisation and so what is obvious to you may not be so to her or him. Use your reflection and analysis sheets to explain *why* your evidence meets the requirements of the standard.

Internal verification

One of the main challenges to the success of NVQs is ensuring that levels of quality are maintained. For the first time, many organisations outside the education sector are heavily involved in supporting those who are working towards a national qualification. For instance, you may well find that your own advisor or assessor is also a work colleague, who has received training in this role. One of the ways in which the quality of the system can be assured is through the process of verification. The first level of verification is internal verification. This is carried out by an internal verifier, who is attached to your assessment centre. The internal verifier randomly samples portfolios in order to ensure that standards are being maintained. She or he is looking to see that assessment decisions are comparable:

- across candidates
- across assessors
- across units

The internal verifier is not there to catch out the assessor – in fact, she or he has no power to overturn assessment decisions. The internal verifier is there to check the quality of the whole programme. We look at their role in more depth in chapter 2.

External verification

The system for external verification is similar to that for internal verification. The external verifier is attached not to your assessment centre but to the awarding body with which you are registered. Again, the external verifier randomly samples portfolios in order to ensure standards are being maintained. She or he is looking to see that the NVQs awarded are comparable:

■ across candidates

■ across assessors

■ across programmes

Again, the external verifier is more interested in the quality of the whole programme in relation to other programmes than in individual cases. For more information on the role of the external verifier see chapter 2.

Award

Finally, when you have been deemed competent in every unit and your portfolio has been internally and externally verified, your assessment centre will apply to the awarding body for your award.

Time

Because of the flexible nature of the qualification, predicting how long it will take is obviously not an exact science. From our experience with candidates, each unit can reasonably be expected to take about six weeks. So, a candidate could complete her or his Management NVQ (at Level 3) in 10.5 months (seven units x 1.5 months). Two factors affect the time it takes a candidate to complete a unit. First, candidates differ as to their speed of completion. This can be due to a number of factors, the most common (in our experience) being pressures at work and the level of motivation to complete the qualification. Although the qualification is flexible in terms of time, a registered candidate has to complete within 36 months of registering, although this varies between awarding bodies.

Another factor is the turnaround time of assessment. Candidates (particularly during the early stages of their NVQ) do not like to start a new unit before they have had feedback from the last one they submitted. A good assessment centre will have a reasonable turnaround time for assessment (for example, two weeks). Unfortunately, some candidates have to wait a lot longer and this obviously affects how long it takes them to complete the qualification. Once completed, your NVQ still has to be verified, and as the external verifier is responsible for many assessment centres, this is often not particularly instant. Once your NVQ has been verified, the awarding body has to generate the relevant paperwork, including your certificate, and the time it takes for this can vary widely across awarding bodies. As a very general guide, as long as you are sufficiently self-motivated and have an efficient assessment centre and awarding body, you can expect to be receiving your NVQ certificate about 12–14 months after registering for your award.

CHAPTER 2

People involved in your NVQ

There are two reasons why we included this chapter. First, we wanted candidates to be clear about the people who would be involved in their NVQ. We have therefore used this chapter to explain who they are and what they do. Our second reason is to assist in raising the quality of NVQ provision. This chapter explains what your rights are with regard to those who support you. If you feel you are not getting the service to which you are entitled, this chapter also describes the options that are open to you.

Advisor

Your advisor will be the most important source of help and advice when it comes to progressing your NVQ. Many organisations now run their NVQ programmes in-house, which means that your advisor may well be a fellow employee. All advisors should be qualified to accredit prior learning – this means that they should already have their Training and Development Lead Body (TDLB) NVQ Unit D36 – as this will be one of the roles they perform. In addition to this, your advisor should be *occupationally competent* in your work area. You can expect your advisor to guide you throughout the whole NVQ process. Don't be afraid to ask advice – that's what your advisor is there for! In particular, your advisor will help you find evidence of any prior learning or achievement that will be relevant to your NVQ. She or he will help you understand the standards and interpret them in ways relevant to your work. When it comes to identifying suitable evidence, your advisor can help you ensure that the evidence you select meets the requirements of the qualification. Should your assessor decide you are 'not yet competent' in any area, your advisor can help you understand the feedback and make the necessary alterations to your portfolio.

You may find yourself in the position of not meeting a specific performance criterion simply because your work role does not cover that area. In this case your advisor can offer you opportunities to gather the necessary evidence through simulation if, in relation to the management standards, this is a viable alternative. Finally, your advisor may offer you ways of demonstrating your knowledge and understanding through, for example, assignments or written tests.

Assessor

Again, as many NVQ programmes are run in-house, your assessor could well be a work colleague. Regardless of whether your assessor is internal or external to your organisation, she or he should be qualified to undertake assessment decisions (by having achieved

TDLB NVQ Units D32 and D33), be occupationally competent in your work area and understand the organisation within which you work. Your assessor should assist you and your advisor in drawing up an assessment plan. It may be that, for some evidence, your assessor will have to observe you in the workplace and this means arranging mutually convenient times. You should expect your assessor to return your portfolio within a mutually agreed time limit. In addition, you should also expect that any assessment decision is supported by thorough feedback. Finally, you have the right to expect your assessor to complete all the relevant documentation regarding the assessment process.

Internal verifier

Your internal verifier will be attached to your assessment centre and should hold TDLB NVQ Unit D34. Your internal verifier plays an important role in quality assurance, as she or he is there to ensure that the assessment decisions are accurate. You may not meet your internal verifier, but, over the course of your NVQ, your portfolio certainly will.

External verifier

Your external verifier is attached to your awarding body and should possess TDLB NVQ Unit D35. You should endeavour to meet your external verifier, if possible, as she or he may have valuable advice in terms of what is happening in other organisations. Again, the external verifier's role is one of quality assurance, monitoring the output of assessment centres.

Work colleagues

If you are going through the NVQ process with colleagues at work, you will find yourself at a considerable advantage over those who have to go it alone. In our experience, those candidates who have formed 'buddy groups' have progressed their NVQ more efficiently than those who work on their own. Informal meetings with colleagues will allow you to share information and ideas. You can learn from the experiences of others and, in return, they can learn from yours. Finally, discussing your NVQ with others has several organisational benefits. For example, you may find that issues you thought were unique to you are, in fact, far more widespread and may therefore require some organisational intervention. In one company, candidates came together to discuss the issue of appraisal, since they had to prove they underwent regular appraisal to meet the requirements of the NVQ. In the absence of a company appraisal system, the candidates between them developed their own and presented it to their senior managers, who approved of the idea and decided to implement it, after minor adaptation.

Assessment centre

Your assessment centre has been awarded the right to administer your NVQ programme on behalf of an awarding body. You should expect your assessment centre to have appropriate resources to do this. For example, it will need to have a suitable management information system that can record and store all the information required by the awarding body and other interested parties, such as funding councils. It will also need systems in place to monitor and ensure the quality of assessment decisions. It should also promote equal and open access to assessment and have suitably competent staff to undertake and verify assessment decisions.

Complaints and appeals

If you are concerned about an assessment decision, your first port of call should be the assessor who made the assessment decision. In our experience, the majority of concerns, when discussed between candidate and assessor, are rectified. However, if the concern cannot be resolved, you should contact your advisor or assessment centre for a copy of their complaints and appeals procedure. Once you have this, you can ensure that your complaint is dealt with. If your concern is about another aspect of your NVQ, you will need to contact whoever is in charge of your programme.

CHAPTER 3

Building your NVQ portfolio

In this chapter we look more closely at how you will achieve your Management NVQ. Your whole qualification will be based on your portfolio of evidence. This will take the form of one or more files which will contain all the evidence you compile over the coming months. This chapter also explains the type of evidence you will be putting into your portfolio.

What is a portfolio of evidence?

This is your own personal collection of evidence that proves that your performance meets the standards of the NVQ. It is likely to take the form of one or more lever arch or ring binder files.

Evidence

The content of your portfolio, put forward in support of the management standards you are attempting to meet, is termed evidence. Evidence should be gathered over the coming months and should correspond with the requirements of each unit, element and performance criterion (PC) of the Management NVQ. You use the evidence you submit to prove your competence. Evidence can take a variety of different forms. We have compiled the following analysis of evidence from our experience with candidates over the past four years.

Types of evidence

Evidence can be classified in two ways: performance evidence and supplementary evidence.

Performance evidence

Whenever possible, you should attempt to produce evidence based on naturally occurring (routine) work activities. The evidence you generate as a result of performing your normal work role is termed performance evidence. It is hard proof of your competence as a manager. Depending on the nature of the evidence, it can be recorded through observation by an advisor or assessor, audio or video recordings, observations by colleagues, subordinates, managers or service users/customers. Here are some examples of performance evidence that candidates have used.

- Reports
- Memos
- Minutes of meetings
- Records of activities
- Notes of action
- Records of projects
- Staff/business objectives
- Business plans
- Contracts
- Budgets
- Quotations
- Purchasing documentation
- Advertising
- Letters
- Job descriptions
- Personnel specifications
- Training plans
- Personal/staff development plans
- Video/audio recordings of your performance
- Induction materials
- Appraisal reports
- References
- Testimonies ('naturally occurring', such as letters from satisfied customers)
- Training evaluation
- Diary/log sheets
- Photographs
- Assessor's written observational analysis sheet (see below)

All the evidence listed above is described as naturally occurring evidence. In other words, it is a by-product of the job you do. Including this evidence in your portfolio would be a matter of photocopying something that already existed or recording a conversation you were going to have anyway. In some cases, it is not practical to include certain evidence in your portfolio. For example, if you are dealing with confidential information, you may not want this information to leave the building. In these cases, your assessor could visit you at work in order to make the assessment decision on the spot. Your assessor would provide you with evidence of this in the form of an observational analysis sheet.

Event route
One important category of performance evidence is that of the event

route. This refers to one whole process or activity which a candidate uses to meet a large chunk of her or his NVQ requirement. The event route focuses on specific areas of your responsibility. It allows you to demonstrate competence against the national standards in a constructive and logical way. Rather than taking a pick-and-mix approach to evidence, the event route allows you to take a specific body of your work and match it against the requirements of the NVQ.

How do I take the event route?
You will need to identify definable areas of your work and then match them against the units of competence that you are undertaking. These areas could include *events* such as special projects, functional processes or certain procedures for which you are responsible. For example:

Special projects could generate the following evidence:

- your remit
- the other people involved and their responsibility
- the resources available
- timescales
- allocation of tasks
- the work that is done
- reporting to the project board or senior managers
- progress and monitoring
- outcomes
- implementation
- monitoring and review

Functional processes that you are involved with or responsible for may include:

- the recruitment and selection process
- budgeting
- planning
- review of products and services
- training and development
- performance review
- negotiations
- employee resourcing
- managing information systems
- disciplinary and grievance procedures
- health and safety

Certain procedures, for example the compilation of a report, could generate the following evidence:

- the need for the report and its purpose
- your remit
- the people involved
- research methodology
- carrying out research
- analysis of findings
- application of findings
- results
- conclusions
- outcomes

Clearly, compiling a report does not result simply in a completed document. The amount of preparation and work undertaken before it is completed is valuable evidence for proving competence. The event route advocates explaining and evidencing the stages of compilation, decisions you have made, the significance of specific aspects of the work, and so on. As long as the evidence is available, the compilation of a report could meet the requirements of several elements across units within the NVQ.

Taking the event route
There are two approaches to the event route. The first is to familiarise yourself with the NVQ standards and the requirements of each unit, and then match them against events in which you have been involved. The second is to identify events, projects and processes in which you have previously been involved, are currently working on or plan to work on in the future, and then to see how they fit into the standards.

The second method is advocated as it makes the NVQ work for you, particularly if you decide to use current or future areas of work. The NVQ standards can be used to guide your decisions or actions and to provide information as to what is expected of you.

Getting advice
Your NVQ advisor or mentor will be able to help you match events against the standards. They may advocate the use of some form of grid or matrix to map the stages of a project or process against a particular element's or unit's requirements and use this as a point of reference when undertaking the work and compiling evidence.

For example, if a candidate is responsible for a project, the different stages of that project would form an event route. The candidate could prove her or his competence in a number of different areas because of the diverse nature of the project. In this case, the candidate would put forward various pieces of evidence associated with the project, for example the initial feasibility study, any contracts or objectives, progress reports and the final evaluation.

Supplementary evidence

When it is not possible to obtain performance evidence, you may support your portfolio with supplementary evidence. This can be generated through questioning by an assessor, testimony reports from managers/colleagues/customers, or simulated training activities. Some examples of evidence, described more fully in the next section, are:

■ Written, audio or video records of candidate's answers to assessor's questions.

■ Testimonies from managers/colleagues/customers given specifically for use in a candidate's NVQ.

■ The output from simulated tasks/activities.

■ Personal statements.

The key thing to remember is that supplementary evidence is just that. It should *support* and *supplement*, not *replace*, your performance evidence.

Special 'NVQ' evidence

Most of the evidence we have referred to so far will already be familiar to you, as items such as reports, letters, minutes of meeting etc. are already part of your job. However, the supplementary evidence we refer to above will be unique to your NVQ. In other words, this 'special' evidence will be generated specifically in order to meet the requirements of the qualification. We have taken the opportunity to label and explain this evidence below.

■ *Observational analysis sheets* – these are a written record of any assessments which take place through observation.

■ *Candidate questioning* – this is a method of generating evidence by questioning the candidate, either face-to-face or in writing.

■ *Witness testimonies* – these are statements made by others as to your performance in the workplace.

■ *Simulations* – these are any training or development opportunities undertaken outside the candidate's normal job that are undertaken purely to meet the requirements of the NVQ. These can include role-playing activities, assignments etc.

■ *Personal statements* – these are accounts by candidates which detail work activities and performance. They are often needed in order to put performance evidence in context, i.e. to provide the assessor with some background or other necessary additional information/explanation.

Evidence requirements

All the evidence you submit must comply with four main specifications. Your assessor will check that your evidence is:

■ valid

■ authentic

■ current

■ sufficient

Validity

Your assessor must be confident that the evidence you put forward relates to the specific standard it is supposed to support. In other words, is it valid? Does it really prove your competence in that specific area? To take an example, one candidate submitted a copy of the *blank* pro-forma sheet she would use for note making in order to prove that she kept records of client contact meetings. Without any notes written on it, this blank pro-forma did not prove that she actually kept records of her meetings with clients, only that this one piece of paper existed! The situation was easily resolved when the assessor undertook an observational assessment of the actual client contact records, kept in the candidate's office.

Authenticity

The assessor is not only concerned about the validity of your evidence, she or he will also be looking for proof that the evidence is yours and can be linked to you. For example, you may put forward as evidence a report that has been authored by your department. In this case, you should highlight your involvement in the production of the report and back this up with a testimony from a relevant 'witness', for example another member of the team who was also involved in producing it.

Currency

As a general rule, evidence you submit in support of the NVQ standards should be no more than two years old. In certain instances, where the standard relates to something that would be classed as non-routine in your particular job, this rule has to be relaxed. Nevertheless, the important point to remember is that you want to prove that you are competent *now*, not at some point in the distant past!

Sufficiency

The final point about evidence is related to its scope. Some of the performance criteria are longitudinal in nature, which means that you have to prove competence over the period of time specified by the standards. Your evidence would obviously have to reflect this and would have to be sufficient to prove your competence over the specified time period.

Portfolio contents

Your portfolio will consist of a number of items:

- the standards;
- your reflection and analysis;
- your evidence;
- feedback from your assessor.

These components should appear in the form of:

■ **The standards themselves**
When submitting your portfolio for assessment you should be sure to include a copy of the standards to which you are to be assessed.

■ **Reflection and analysis sheets**
You will have to write a justification supporting why your evidence meets the standards required by the NVQ. This is done on a reflection and analysis sheet, on a PC by PC basis. For an example of a completed reflection and analysis sheet, see Appendix 1.

■ **Evidence referencing system**
Your reflection and analysis will refer to a number of different types of evidence, some of which you will want to include in your portfolio (not all evidence may be included in your portfolio since some of it may be assessed by observational assessment). Given the amount of evidence needed to meet the requirements of the NVQ, an evidence referencing system is obviously essential. How you design it is up to you, but bear in mind that a simple system is most effective. As assessors, we know how frustrating it is to be presented with a portfolio whose referencing system is illogical and inaccurate. A straightforward numbering system (1, 2, 3 etc.) works well and any evidence that needs to be added later can be labelled 1a, 1b, 1c, and so on. Dividers can be used to separate evidence at suitable intervals (items 1–10, 11–20, 21–30, etc.).

■ **Cross-referencing**
Cross-referencing refers to the ability of one piece of evidence to meet the requirements of more than one performance criterion. You should make use of cross-referencing at every available opportunity. It is surprising how, with a little thought, the amount of evidence you submit can be reduced in this way. When you have identified a piece of evidence for a particular PC/element/unit, flick through forthcoming PCs, elements and units to make sure there isn't something more relevant that would serve both purposes. Some assessors have been complaining of increased petrol costs and back pain brought about by the sheer size of the NVQ portfolios they have to transport and assess! Obviously, reducing the amount of evidence submitted makes things simpler both for you and for your assessor.

■ **Feedback sheets**
Your assessor will complete assessment forms that detail her/his decision (competent, not yet competent, insufficient evidence) on each element and unit you put forward for assessment. This feedback may well be augmented by a personal visit by your assessor. Different people have different ways of working, but you must always get feedback in writing as to why you were deemed competent (or not yet competent). We have included an example of a completed assessor's feedback sheet in Appendix 2.

Part Two Unit Interpretations and How to Use Them

The second part of this book focuses on your achievement of the Management NVQ at Level 3. Each chapter deals with one unit of the qualification, and is split up into the associated elements and performance criteria as laid down by the MCI management standards. An example of an interpretation from this book is given below, along with a full explanation of each section.

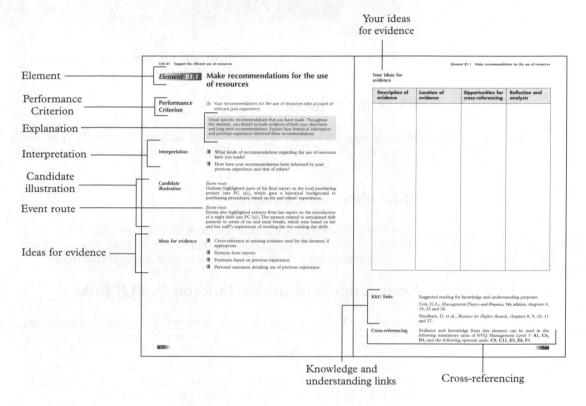

Element

Performance Criterion

Explanation

Interpretation

Candidate illustration

Event route

Ideas for evidence

Your ideas for evidence

Knowledge and understanding links

Cross-referencing

Explanation

An explanation of each performance criterion appears in a tinted panel. The purpose of this explanation is to help you focus on relevant evidence that will enable you to meet the requirements of the standard. It also raises the necessary points that you need to cover in your reflection and analysis.

Interpretation

To help you interpret the standard in ways applicable and relevant to your job, we have listed a number of questions you may like to ask yourself. Answering these questions through the use of evidence and analysis will ensure you meet the requirements of the performance criterion.

Candidate illustration

Through our involvement with NVQ candidates we have been able to illustrate how other people have met the requirements of the qualification. For continuity we have drawn from the experiences and portfolios of two candidates: Emma and Graham. We have chosen them to represent the different organisations in which candidates work. Emma works as a production supervisor for a manufacturing organisation in the private sector, while Graham is a residential care manager working in the public sector.

Event route

Sometimes the evidence to which we refer is part of an event route. For more information on this type of evidence see page 19.

Ideas for evidence

To assist your processes of evidence identification and collection, we have given some examples of evidence that may be useful, for each performance criterion listed.

Your ideas for evidence

Experience shows that candidates benefit from jotting down their ideas for evidence as they think of them. To facilitate this, we have included a table for you to use while working through this book.

Knowledge and understanding (K&U) links

Getting an NVQ is not just about proving *what* you do. You also need to demonstrate *why* you do it. Different providers of NVQs have different ways of testing your underpinning knowledge and understanding. However, to assist your reading and development, we have cross-referenced each performance criterion to relevant parts of three leading business and management texts. These are:

■ Cole, G.A., 1996, *Management: Theory and Practice*, 5th edition, Letts Educational, London.

■ Mullins, L.J., 1996, *Management and Organisational Behaviour*, 4th edition, Pitman Publishing, London.

■ Needham, D., Dransfield, R. Harris, R., and Coles, M., 1995, *Business for Higher Awards*, Heinemann, Oxford.

We recommend that you have regular access to at least one of these texts.

Cross-referencing

As every portfolio is unique, so too are the opportunities for cross-referencing. Nevertheless, evidence put forward in support of some performance criteria will often be suitable for others and we have listed these opportunities for cross-referencing.

CHAPTER 4

Maintain activities to meet requirements

Element A1.1 Maintain work activities to meet requirements

Performance Criterion

(a) *You agree requirements with customers in sufficient detail to allow work to be planned.*

> To meet the requirements of this PC you will need to detail how customer requirements are identified in your work role. Explain any processes or standardised documents that you may use with customers. Illustrate your actions with specific examples. Focus on how the information is used to plan the work involved. Throughout this element, customer requirements should relate to quality, quantity, delivery, and health and safety. Customers could be either internal (such as other departments who use your services) or external.

Interpretation

◾ What kind of responsibility do you have for agreeing customer requirements?

◾ How are requirements identified?

◾ How are requirements used to plan work?

Candidate illustration

Event route
To meet the requirements of this element, Graham focused on the care planning he does with service users. He submitted a detailed personal statement setting the context and explaining individual care plans, completed in discussion with residents and their families and other agencies involved in the provision of care. Two examples of care plans were submitted as evidence. The relevant sections detailing residents' dietary and medical requirements were highlighted and labelled in support of this performance criterion.

Event route
Part of Emma's role was to set and agree production standards for her team, which manufactures a range of circuit boards used in electrical appliances by the organisation. Targets are based on customer orders, overall organisational production targets and, at a local level, the requirements of the other production teams involved in the manufacturing process. For the purposes of the NVQ, the other teams who required the circuit boards were defined as internal customers. Emma included minutes of meetings with other team leaders where numbers and targets were agreed.

Ideas for evidence

◾ Reports of internal or external customer requirements.

◾ Minutes of meetings.

◾ Contracts.

◾ Agreed plans.

◾ Memos.

◾ Personal statement explaining background.

Your ideas for evidence

Description of evidence	Location of evidence	Opportunities for cross-referencing	Reflection and analysis

K&U links

Suggested reading for knowledge and understanding purposes:

Cole, G.A., *Management: Theory and Practice*, 5th edition, chapters 6, 19 and 21.

Mullins, L.J., *Management and Organisational Behaviour*, 4th edition, chapter 9.

Needham, D. et al., *Business for Higher Awards*, chapter 11.

Cross-referencing

Evidence and knowledge from this element can be used in the following mandatory units of NVQ Management Level 3: **B1**, **C4**, **D1**; and the following optional units: **C12**, **F5**.

Element A1.1   Maintain work activities to meet requirements

Performance Criterion

(b) You explain requirements to relevant people in sufficient detail and at an appropriate level and pace.

> You can link to PC (a), if appropriate. Explain who relevant people are, in your situation. They should include one of the following: team members, peers, higher-level manager, or sponsors and external people. Focus on the level of detail that you explain. Illustrate how you gauge the most effective means of communicating, with the individuals involved.

Interpretation

- Who are the other people involved?
- How do you use your knowledge of these people to identify appropriate means of communicating with them?
- How much detail do they require?

Candidate illustration

Event route
Throughout the care-planning process, Graham had to liaise with individual residents' relatives and people from other organisations involved, including general practitioners, social services and the local health authority. Aspects of the care plan were highlighted to illustrate their involvement. Graham also submitted examples of correspondence with other people involved.

Event route
While setting production targets, Emma routinely met with her team to explain requirements, plan work, and obtain their views and suggestions. Examples of minutes of these meetings were submitted as evidence. In her analysis Emma explained her approach to team briefing, illustrating her knowledge of how to provide the team with clear information.

Ideas for evidence

- Cross-reference to existing evidence, if appropriate.
- Examples of correspondence with the relevant people.
- Minutes of meetings.
- Other relevant communication:
  - presentation notes and slides;
  - letters;
  - emails etc.

Your ideas for evidence

Description of evidence	Location of evidence	Opportunities for cross-referencing	Reflection and analysis

K&U links Suggested reading for knowledge and understanding purposes:

Cole, G.A., *Management: Theory and Practice*, 5th edition, chapters 6, 19 and 21.

Mullins, L.J., *Management and Organisational Behaviour*, 4th edition, chapters 9 and 16.

Needham, D. et al., *Business for Higher Awards*, chapters 10 and 11.

Cross-referencing Evidence and knowledge from this element can be used in the following mandatory units of NVQ Management Level 3: **B1, C4, D1**; and the following optional units: **C12, F5**.

Element A1.1 Maintain work activities to meet requirements

Performance Criterion

(c) You confirm with relevant people their understanding of, and commitment to, meeting requirements.

> Explain how you ensure that requirements, and the work activities needed to meet them, have been understood by the others involved. Give examples where you have confirmed understanding and detail your methods of doing this. Focus on how this encourages commitment to, and involvement in, work activities.

Interpretation

- Why is it important to ensure understanding?
- How do you do this?
- What impact does this have on meeting requirements?

Candidate illustration

Event route
Graham was again able to highlight aspects of the care-planning documents where other agencies and individuals were involved. Where a direct input from external sources was needed, the people involved were required to read the plan, then sign it to agree to provide service. Graham explained the process with a personal statement and highlighted the relevant parts of the care plans as evidence.

Event route
Emma cross-referenced to the minutes of meetings with her team used in PC (b) of this element. She highlighted instances where individuals had sought clarification of requirements through discussion with the team and through questioning.

Ideas for evidence

- Cross-reference to existing evidence, if appropriate.
- Minutes of meetings where requirements have been clarified.
- Reports of discussions with others involved.
- Supervision documentation.

Your ideas for evidence

Description of evidence	Location of evidence	Opportunities for cross-referencing	Reflection and analysis

K&U links

Suggested reading for knowledge and understanding purposes:

Cole, G.A., *Management: Theory and Practice*, 5th edition, chapters 6, 19 and 21.

Mullins, L.J., *Management and Organisational Behaviour*, 4th edition, chapters 9 and 16.

Needham, D. et al., *Business for Higher Awards*, chapters 10 and 11.

Cross-referencing

Evidence and knowledge from this element can be used in the following mandatory units of NVQ Management Level 3: **B1, C4, D1**; and the following optional units: **C12, F5**.

Element A1.1 Maintain work activities to meet requirements

Performance Criterion

(d) Your monitoring of your team's work takes place at appropriate intervals and complies with your organisation's procedures.

> You will have to detail specific examples of your monitoring process. Explain the timescales involved. Examine the procedures involved and provide information on your actions.

Interpretation

- Is monitoring a routine part of your job role?
- Do you use your own monitoring system?
- Do you use organisational documentation and procedures for monitoring purposes?
- How does monitoring of your team's work occur?

Candidate illustration

Event route

As part of the care-planning process, residents are each allocated a key worker, who is primarily responsible for the provision of care in the individual's care plan. Graham included examples of supervision documentation, completed in accordance with the organisation's requirements, that reviewed the provision of care by the key worker. Relevant aspects of the documents were highlighted and Graham explained specific issues in his analysis of the evidence. He also explained the organisational policy and procedures concerning staff supervision.

Event route

Emma received daily statistics detailing the outputs of her teams, faulty components and production times. Where targets were not met, Emma discussed the reasons for this with the staff involved, noting action to be taken and the timescales required. These discussions were recorded using standardised documents and kept as records of agreements between staff and supervisor. Examples were submitted as evidence here.

Ideas for evidence

- Supervision documentation.
- Notes of conversations and meetings with staff.
- Details of the timescales involved and their significance.

Your ideas for evidence

Description of evidence	Location of evidence	Opportunities for cross-referencing	Reflection and analysis

K&U links

Suggested reading for knowledge and understanding purposes:

Cole, G.A., *Management: Theory and Practice,* 5th edition, chapters 6, 19 and 21.

Mullins, L.J., *Management and Organisational Behaviour,* 4th edition, chapters 9 and 16.

Needham, D. et al., *Business for Higher Awards*, chapters 10 and 11.

Cross-referencing

Evidence and knowledge from this element can be used in the following mandatory units of NVQ Management Level 3: **B1, C4, D1**; and the following optional units: **C12, F5**.

| Element A1.1 | # Maintain work activities to meet requirements |

Performance Criterion

(e) *The work under your control normally meets agreed requirements.*

> You could link to PC (d), if appropriate. In maintaining work activities, explain how you ensure that the work undertaken is in line with requirements in terms of quality, quantity, delivery, and health and safety.

Interpretation

- How do you know whether work activities are meeting requirements?
- How do agreed requirements impact on work activities?
- What actions do you take to maintain standards of work?

Candidate illustration

Event route

Both Graham and Emma cross-referenced to the evidence used for PC (d). Graham explained the purposes of supervision in his analysis and obtained a witness testimony from his manager confirming that agreed requirements were normally met. Emma explained that, normally, targets are met or bettered. She submitted internally published statistics confirming her statement.

Ideas for evidence

- Cross-reference to existing evidence used in this element, if appropriate.
- Statistics or reports confirming that requirements have been met.
- Witness testimony from others involved.

Your ideas for evidence

Description of evidence	Location of evidence	Opportunities for cross-referencing	Reflection and analysis

K&U links

Suggested reading for knowledge and understanding purposes:

Cole, G.A., *Management: Theory and Practice*, 5th edition, chapters 6, 19 and 21.

Mullins, L.J., *Management and Organisational Behaviour*, 4th edition, chapters 9 and 16.

Needham, D. et al., *Business for Higher Awards*, chapters 10 and 11.

Cross-referencing

Evidence and knowledge from this element can be used in the following mandatory units of NVQ Management Level 3: **B1**, **C4**, **D1**; and the following optional units: **C12**, **F5**.

Element A1.1	# Maintain work activities to meet requirements

Performance Criterion

(f) *When products, services and processes do not meet agreed requirements, you take prompt and effective corrective action.*

> We recommend that you link to previous performance criteria in this element, if possible. Focus on specific instances where agreed requirements have not been met. Explain the significance of the instance and detail the steps you have taken to rectify the situation.

Interpretation

▪ When have products, services and processes not met agreed requirements?

▪ Why was this?

▪ What were the implications?

▪ What actions did you take?

▪ What was the end result?

Candidate illustration

Event route

Graham highlighted an instance where a resident's dietary requirements were not being met. He explained the importance of the care plan in identifying such requirements, as this particular resident was diabetic. In this instance, Graham arranged to meet with the resident's key worker to seek explanations for the error, which was corrected through a memo to catering staff. Notes of the discussion with the key worker were also included.

Event route

Emma highlighted an instance where daily production targets were not met owing to staff shortage through illness. Emma was able to employ a replacement agency worker, on a temporary basis, to cover for the shortage. Her evidence consisted of the statistical printout highlighting the production figures. She also included the agency's invoice for the temporary worker.

Ideas for evidence

▪ Details of the circumstances surrounding the occurrence:
  – reports;
  – memos;
  – notes of conversations.

▪ Minutes of meetings where corrective action has been planned.

▪ Examples of corrective action taken.

Your ideas for evidence

Description of evidence	Location of evidence	Opportunities for cross-referencing	Reflection and analysis

K&U links

Suggested reading for knowledge and understanding purposes:

Cole, G.A., *Management: Theory and Practice,* 5th edition, chapters 6, 19 and 21.

Mullins, L.J., *Management and Organisational Behaviour,* 4th edition, chapters 9 and 16.

Needham, D. et al., *Business for Higher Awards,* chapters 10, 11 and 28.

Cross-referencing

Evidence and knowledge from this element can be used in the following mandatory units of NVQ Management Level 3: **B1, C4, D1**; and the following optional units: **C12, F5**.

Element A1.1   Maintain work activities to meet requirements

Performance Criterion

(g) Records relating to the work under your control are complete, accurate and in line with your organisation's procedures.

> Link to previous performance criteria from this element, if appropriate. Explain the records that you submit as evidence. Detail their purpose and function in recording and providing information relating to your work. Highlight any organisational procedures that require records to be kept and their impact on your work activities.

Interpretation

- What kinds of records are kept?
- What are they used for?
- Why is accuracy important?
- Which organisational procedures impact on record keeping?

Candidate illustration

Event route
Graham cross-referenced to the standardised supervision records used in PC (d). He explained the purpose of supervision, and the significance of the issues discussed, in his analysis of evidence.

Event route
Emma cross-referenced to the statistics used in PC (d). She explained what they were used for and the information they provided in her analysis of evidence.

Ideas for evidence

- Examples of records kept.
- Personal statement explaining their significance and use.
- Details of organisational procedures that require record keeping.

Your ideas for evidence

Description of evidence	Location of evidence	Opportunities for cross-referencing	Reflection and analysis

K&U links

Suggested reading for knowledge and understanding purposes:

Cole, G.A., *Management: Theory and Practice,* 5th edition, chapters 6, 19 and 21.

Mullins, L.J., *Management and Organisational Behaviour,* 4th edition, chapters 9 and 16.

Needham, D. et al., *Business for Higher Awards,* chapters 10, 11, 17, 18 and 25.

Cross-referencing

Evidence and knowledge from this element can be used in the following mandatory units of NVQ Management Level 3: **B1**, **C4**, **D1**; and the following optional units: **C12**, **F5**.

Element A1.1   Maintain work activities to meet requirements

Performance Criterion

(h) You give opportunities to relevant people to make recommendations for improving work activities.

> Link to evidence used for previous performance criteria in this element, if appropriate. Highlight actions you have taken to ensure that other people involved in your work are given opportunities to make suggestions for improvement. Explain the circumstances, and detail the kinds of suggestions made and the action taken based on those suggestions. Relevant people should include one of the following: team members, peers, higher-level managers, or sponsors and external people.

Interpretation

- How have you provided these kinds of opportunities?
- Who was involved?
- What kinds of suggestions were made?
- What actions were taken?
- How were the improvements made?

Candidate illustration

Event route
Graham again cross-referenced to the supervision documentation originally used as evidence for PC (d). He highlighted sections of the completed documentation where staff had proposed courses of action and made suggestions for improvement to their working practices. In his analysis, Graham explained his approach to supervision and stated that he actively sought input from staff to maintain continuous improvement.

Event route
Emma cross-referenced to the minutes of the team-briefing meetings originally used as evidence for PC (a). She highlighted parts of the minutes where suggestions had been made and accepted concerning break times and shift handovers.

Ideas for evidence

- Cross-reference to existing evidence, if appropriate.
- Examples of supervision notes where suggestions have been made.
- Minutes of meetings where suggestions and recommendations have been made.
- Reports received from people detailing recommendations for improvement.

Your ideas for evidence

Description of evidence	Location of evidence	Opportunities for cross-referencing	Reflection and analysis

K&U links   Suggested reading for knowledge and understanding purposes:

Cole, G.A., *Management: Theory and Practice,* 5th edition, chapters 6, 19 and 21.

Mullins, L.J., *Management and Organisational Behaviour,* 4th edition, chapters 9 and 16.

Needham, D. et al., *Business for Higher Awards,* chapters 10 and 11.

Cross-referencing   Evidence and knowledge from this element can be used in the following mandatory units of NVQ Management Level 3: **B1, D1**; and the following optional units: **C9, F5, F7**.

Element A1.2	# Maintain healthy, safe and productive working conditions

Performance Criterion

(a) *You inform relevant people about their legal and organisational responsibilities for maintaining healthy, safe and productive working conditions.*

> Explain your responsibility for maintaining a healthy, safe and productive working environment. Detail how you communicate the shared responsibility for health and safety issues to relevant people, and give examples of your actions. Relevant people should include the following throughout this element: team members, peers, higher-level managers, or sponsors and external people.

Interpretation

■ What are people's responsibilities regarding the maintenance of healthy, safe and productive working conditions?

■ Under what circumstances have you informed them of these responsibilities?

■ How has this been done?

Candidate illustration

Event route
Graham detailed his responsibilities for an internal health and safety audit prior to an external local government inspection of his residential home. He designed a programme of events for the audit, beginning with briefing sessions to all staff regarding the legal requirements of health and safety legislation and the concepts of shared responsibility and risk assessment. His notes and the overhead transparencies used for his briefings were submitted as evidence.

Event route
Emma focused on her responsibility regarding the induction process for new employees. She explained in her analysis that health and safety issues were of paramount importance for those working with machinery on the shop floor. She included notes made during the induction of a new employee using standardised documentation relating to health and safety.

Ideas for evidence

■ Minutes of briefings given concerning health and safety.

■ Induction processes.

■ Observation of notices posted for staff regarding health and safety issues.

■ Memos and correspondence sent to people regarding health and safety.

Your ideas for evidence

Description of evidence	Location of evidence	Opportunities for cross-referencing	Reflection and analysis

K&U links

Suggested reading for knowledge and understanding purposes:

Cole, G.A., *Management: Theory and Practice,* 5th edition, chapter 50, pp. 403–4.

Any health and safety/risk assessment text.

Mullins, L.J., *Management and Organisational Behaviour,* 4th edition, chapter 15.

Needham, D. et al., *Business for Higher Awards,* chapter 24.

Cross-referencing

Evidence and knowledge from this element can be used in the following mandatory units of NVQ Management Level 3: **B1**, **D1**; and the following optional units: **C9**, **F5**, **F7**.

Element A1.2	# Maintain healthy, safe and productive working conditions

Performance Criterion

(b) You give sufficient support to relevant people to ensure they are able to work in a healthy, safe and productive way.

> Detail an incident where you have supported people in maintaining a healthy, safe and productive working environment. Explain the circumstances and the actions that you took.

Interpretation

- How have you given this kind of support?
- What actions were taken?
- How did the actions support the others involved?
- How was the work environment maintained/improved?

Candidate illustration

Event route
Throughout the health and safety audit process, Graham identified areas for improvement. These were recorded using audit documentation and discussed with those involved in the areas of work to be improved. The audit documentation was submitted as evidence, together with notes taken during interviews with those concerned to identify the courses of action to be taken.

Event route
Emma submitted completed induction records for two members of staff which detailed the information they had been given and the training and development they had been offered to assist their understanding of health and safety issues.

Ideas for evidence

- Notes of meetings where you have provided this level of support.
- Audit documents identifying and recording the provision of support to assist improvements in health and safety and the working environment.
- Details of the support provided:
  - training and development;
  - resources;
  - information.

Your ideas for evidence

Description of evidence	Location of evidence	Opportunities for cross-referencing	Reflection and analysis

K&U links

Suggested reading for knowledge and understanding purposes:

Cole, G.A., *Management: Theory and Practice*, 5th edition, chapter 50, pp. 403–4.

Any health and safety/risk assessment text.

Mullins, L.J., *Management and Organisational Behaviour*, 4th edition, chapter 15.

Needham, D. et al., *Business for Higher Awards*, chapter 24.

Cross-referencing

Evidence and knowledge from this element can be used in the following mandatory units of NVQ Management Level 3: **B1**, **D1**; and the following optional units: **C9**, **F5**, **F7**.

Element A1.2   Maintain healthy, safe and productive working conditions

Performance Criterion

(c) *You give opportunities to relevant people to make recommendations for improving working conditions.*

> Detail, with examples, how these opportunities have been provided. They may be routine or non-routine occurrences within your organisation. Explain specific recommendations and the circumstances surrounding them.

Interpretation

▪ How have you provided these kinds of opportunities?

▪ Who was involved?

▪ What kinds of recommendations were made?

▪ What action was taken?

▪ How were improvements made?

Candidate illustration

Event route
Throughout the health and safety audit process, Graham had meetings with all staff groups to discuss the working implications for the improvements to be made regarding health and safety. At every meeting, Graham invited input from staff through written suggestion or verbal discussion. He submitted minutes of some of the briefings where recommendations had been made and also included an example of a written suggestion received from a member of staff.

Event route
Emma recorded all staff suggestions made during the induction process on standard induction documents. She submitted two examples where recommendations for improvements to health and safety practices had been made by new members of staff, based on their previous employment. Emma explained in her analysis that she had already sought these kinds of recommendations from all staff.

Ideas for evidence

▪ Minutes of meetings where these kinds of recommendations have been made.

▪ Notes of supervision and induction sessions where recommendations have been made.

▪ Written recommendations received from staff.

Your ideas for evidence

Description of evidence	Location of evidence	Opportunities for cross-referencing	Reflection and analysis

K&U links

Suggested reading for knowledge and understanding purposes:

Cole, G.A., *Management: Theory and Practice*, 5th edition, chapter 50, pp. 403–4.

Any health and safety/risk assessment text.

Mullins, L.J., *Management and Organisational Behaviour*, 4th edition, chapter 15.

Needham, D. et al., *Business for Higher Awards*, chapter 24.

Cross-referencing

Evidence and knowledge from this element can be used in the following mandatory units of NVQ Management Level 3: **B1**, **D1**; and the following optional units: **C9**, **F5**, **F7**.

Element A1.2	# Maintain healthy, safe and productive working conditions

Performance Criterion

(d) *Working conditions under your control conform to organisational and legal requirements.*

> Link to PC (e) of this element, if appropriate. Explain the organisational and legal requirements that impact on the working environment for which you are responsible. Aspects of the working environment should include two of the following throughout this element: physical environment, equipment, materials and working procedures. Detail actions you have taken to ensure compliance with these requirements.

Interpretation

■ What requirements impact on your responsibilities to ensure healthy, safe and productive working conditions?

■ How do you ensure compliance with these requirements?

■ What actions have you taken?

Candidate illustration

Event route
Graham used the internal audit to highlight best practice observed by staff concerning health and safety. He used the external audit document as evidence, highlighting the relevant sections that related to organisational and legal requirements.

Event route
Emma submitted some of her own supervision records, where she was supervised by her line manager. She highlighted instances where health and safety inspections had confirmed that the working conditions for which she was responsible met legal and internal requirements.

Ideas for evidence

■ Records and documents completed following health and safety inspections.

■ Personal statement confirming health and safety practices.

■ Witness testimony from others involved.

Your ideas for evidence

Description of evidence	Location of evidence	Opportunities for cross-referencing	Reflection and analysis

K&U links

Suggested reading for knowledge and understanding purposes:

Cole, G.A., *Management: Theory and Practice*, 5th edition, chapter 50, pp. 403–4.

Any health and safety/risk assessment text.

Mullins, L.J., *Management and Organisational Behaviour*, 4th edition, chapter 15.

Needham, D. et al., *Business for Higher Awards*, chapter 24.

Cross-referencing

Evidence and knowledge from this element can be used in the following mandatory units of NVQ Management Level 3: **B1**, **D1**; and the following optional units: **C9**, **F5**, **F7**.

Element A1.2 — Maintain healthy, safe and productive working conditions

Performance Criterion

(e) Working conditions under your control are as conducive to the work activity as possible within organisational constraints.

> Explain how your working environment is designed to support the work activities undertaken. Detail how this has been established and your role in maintaining it. Highlight any organisational constraints that you have had to comply with.

Interpretation

◾ How does the work environment for which you are responsible support the work roles carried out?

◾ What is your role in maintaining or improving the work environment?

◾ How have your actions been in line with organisational constraints?

Candidate illustration

Event route
Graham was again able to cross-reference to the internal health and safety audit documentation he had completed (see PC (a) of this element). He highlighted relevant sections detailing the working environment and conditions. Graham also submitted a personal report describing the organisational constraints that related to the working environment, including both budgetary and human resource constraints.

Event route
Emma focused on the physical environment when meeting the requirements of this PC. She invited her NVQ assessor to observe the shop floor and confirm that it was designed for the manufacturing process being undertaken. In addition, she submitted several suggestions for improvement received from staff that had to be rejected because of financial constraints on the organisation.

Ideas for evidence

◾ Cross-reference to existing evidence, if appropriate.

◾ Details of the physical environment, equipment used, material used and the working procedures employed.

◾ Internal inspection or audit documentation.

◾ External inspection or audit documentation.

◾ Witness testimony from those working in the environment concerned.

◾ Observational assessment by your NVQ assessor.

Your ideas for evidence

Description of evidence	Location of evidence	Opportunities for cross-referencing	Reflection and analysis

K&U links   Suggested reading for knowledge and understanding purposes:

Cole, G.A., *Management: Theory and Practice*, 5th edition, chapter 50, pp. 403–4.

Any health and safety/risk assessment text.

Mullins, L.J., *Management and Organisational Behaviour*, 4th edition, chapter 15.

Needham, D. et al., *Business for Higher Awards*, chapter 24.

Cross-referencing   Evidence and knowledge from this element can be used in the following mandatory units of NVQ Management Level 3: **B1**, **D1**; and the following optional units: **C9**, **F5**, **F7**.

Element A1.2 Maintain healthy, safe and productive working conditions

Performance Criterion

(f) *You respond to breaches in health and safety requirements in ways which are prompt and consistent with organisational and legal requirements.*

> Provide examples of specific breaches of health and safety requirements. Explain how you responded and the circumstances behind your involvement. Detail the timescales involved and any organisational and legal requirements that informed your actions.

Interpretation

▪ Under what circumstances have breaches in health and safety requirements occurred?

▪ What actions have you taken?

▪ What were the timescales involved?

▪ Which organisational and legal requirements informed your actions?

Candidate illustration

Event route
Graham highlighted the internal health and safety audit documentation to show potential hazards in the work environment. These concerned the positioning of equipment in the office and in the kitchens. Proposed action and timescales were also included. Graham explained the potential hazards in his analysis and justified the actions taken.

Event route
Emma detailed an accident on the shop floor when an employee slipped on a wet surface. She submitted evidence of her entry into the accident book (a legal requirement) and detailed her actions in assisting the injured staff member to receive medical help (in line with organisational guidelines).

Ideas for evidence

▪ Internal audit or inspection documentation.

▪ External audit or inspection documentation.

▪ Reports relating to breaches in health and safety requirements.

▪ Extracts from an accident book or log.

Your ideas for evidence

Description of evidence	Location of evidence	Opportunities for cross-referencing	Reflection and analysis

K&U links   Suggested reading for knowledge and understanding purposes:

Cole, G.A., *Management: Theory and Practice*, 5th edition, chapter 50, pp. 403–4.

Any health and safety/risk assessment text.

Mullins, L.J., *Management and Organisational Behaviour*, 4th edition, chapter 15.

Needham, D. et al., *Business for Higher Awards*, chapter 24.

Cross-referencing   Evidence and knowledge from this element can be used in the following mandatory units of NVQ Management Level 3: **B1**, **D1**; and the following optional units: **C9**, **F5**, **F7**.

Element *A1.2*	**Maintain healthy, safe and productive working conditions**

Performance Criterion

(g) You make recommendations for improving working conditions clearly and promptly to relevant people.

> Link to evidence used for previous performance criteria within this element, if appropriate. Detail specific instances where you have made these kinds of recommendations. Explain the timescales involved. Relevant people should include two of the following: team members, peers, higher-level managers, or sponsors and external people.

Interpretation

- Under what circumstances have you made recommendations?
- To whom were they made?
- What were the timescales involved?
- How were the recommendations presented?

Candidate illustration

Event route
As a result of the internal health and safety audit, Graham made recommendations to his line manager in the form of a written report. Graham highlighted the recommendations made in the report, which focused on procedures for storing medicines and drugs and revising the kitchen layout to improve health and hygiene in line with legal requirements. Before Graham submitted the report, he asked his health and safety inspector to clarify that the recommendations contained within it were appropriate.

Event route
Emma included two memos sent to senior management highlighting the need for modernisation of some of the machinery used in the production process. As a result of the memos, Emma was asked to report in more detail on the cost implications of the recommendations and to present a written action plan to support their implementation. These were also submitted as evidence.

Ideas for evidence

- Examples of recommendations made:
  – memos;
  – reports;
  – presentations;
  – briefing papers.

- Personal statement explaining who the relevant people were and the significance of the timescales involved.

Your ideas for evidence

Description of evidence	Location of evidence	Opportunities for cross-referencing	Reflection and analysis

K&U links

Suggested reading for knowledge and understanding purposes:

Cole, G.A., *Management: Theory and Practice*, 5th edition, chapter 50, pp. 403–4.

Any health and safety/risk assessment text.

Mullins, L.J., *Management and Organisational Behaviour*, 4th edition, chapter 15.

Needham, D. et al., *Business for Higher Awards*, chapter 24.

Cross-referencing

Evidence and knowledge from this element can be used in the following mandatory units of NVQ Management Level 3: **B1, D1**; and the following optional units: **C9, F5, F7**.

Element A1.2	# Maintain healthy, safe and productive working conditions

Performance Criterion

(h) Your records relating to health and safety and working conditions are complete, accurate, and comply with organisational and legal requirements.

> Link to previous performance criteria for this element, if appropriate. Explain the records that you submit as evidence. Detail their purpose and function in recording and providing information relating to health and safety issues. Highlight any organisational and legal requirements that require records to be kept.

Interpretation

- What kinds of records are kept?
- What are they used for?
- Why is accuracy important?
- Which organisational and legal requirements impact on this kind of record keeping?

Candidate illustration

Event route
Both Graham and Emma were able to cross-reference to existing evidence used for this element: the extract from the accident book used by Emma in PC (f), and the audit documentation completed by Graham and used throughout this element. In their analyses, Graham and Emma explained the documentation and its significance, and outlined the organisational and legal requirements that inform the content of their records.

Ideas for evidence

- Cross-reference to existing evidence used in this element, if appropriate.
- Examples of records submitted.
- Personal statement explaining relevant organisational and legal requirements.

Your ideas for evidence

Description of evidence	Location of evidence	Opportunities for cross-referencing	Reflection and analysis

K&U links

Suggested reading for knowledge and understanding purposes:

Cole, G.A., *Management: Theory and Practice*, 5th edition, chapter 50, pp. 403–4.

Any health and safety/risk assessment text.

Mullins, L.J., *Management and Organisational Behaviour*, 4th edition, chapter 15.

Needham, D. et al., *Business for Higher Awards*, chapter 24.

Cross-referencing

Evidence and knowledge from this element can be used in the following mandatory units of NVQ Management Level 3: **B1**, **D1**; and the following optional units: **C9**, **F5**, **F7**.

Make recommendations for improvements to work activities

Performance Criterion

(a) *You provide opportunities for relevant people to suggest ways of improving activities.*

Link to evidence used for previous elements in this unit, if appropriate. Highlight actions you have taken to ensure that other people involved in your work are given opportunities to make suggestions for improvement. Explain the circumstances, and detail the kinds of suggestions made and the actions taken based on those suggestions. Relevant people must include two of the following throughout this element: team members, peers, higher-level managers, or sponsors and specialists.

Interpretation

▌ How have you provided these kinds of opportunities?

▌ Who was involved?

▌ What kinds of suggestions were made?

▌ What action was taken?

▌ How were improvements made?

Candidate illustration

Event route
Graham focused on a report he had produced for senior management making recommendations for revising the in-house induction process for new staff. He used the report and supporting material to meet the requirements of the whole element, annotating the report in support of specific performance criteria.

The background to the report detailed the consultation that Graham had undertaken to obtain views from staff and the central personnel department. He annotated this part of the report and clearly explained his actions in his analysis.

Event route
Emma also focused on a specific feasibility study she had undertaken concerning extending shift patterns to provide 24-hour production in times of high demand. She was able to use the final project report and evidence of activities undertaken throughout the element.

In this case, her evidence consisted of two of the appendices to the final project report, together with the section of the main report to which they referred. The appendices were minutes of two meetings that Emma had convened and chaired. The first detailed a meeting with other managers and supervisors who would be affected by the changes. The second was a team meeting where the project was announced and feedback requested.

Ideas for evidence ▮ Details of specific improvements to work activities with which you have been involved:
– reports;
– briefing documents;
– projects.

▮ Minutes of meetings where you have consulted the relevant people.

▮ Notes of discussions.

▮ Supervision documentation.

Your ideas for evidence

Description of evidence	Location of evidence	Opportunities for cross-referencing	Reflection and analysis

K&U links Suggested reading for knowledge and understanding purposes:

Cole, G.A., *Management: Theory and Practice*, 5th edition, chapters 19, 21 and 26.

Mullins, L.J., *Management and Organisational Behaviour*, 4th edition, chapters 7, 9 and 13.

Needham, D. et al., *Business for Higher Awards*, chapters 10 and 11.

Cross-referencing Evidence and knowledge from this element can be used in the following mandatory units of NVQ Management Level 3: **B1**, **C4**, **D1**; and the following optional units: **C9**, **C12**, **C15**, **E5**, **E8**, **F5**.

Element A1.3	# Make recommendations for improvements to work activities

Performance Criterion

(b) Your recommendations for improvements to activities are based on sufficient, valid and reliable information.

> Evidence and explain the kinds of information that you use to inform your recommendations for improvements to work activities. Highlight your sources of information and explain how you check for validity and reliability.

Interpretation

▌ What kinds of information do you use to make these kinds of recommendations?

▌ How do you check your information for accuracy?

Candidate illustration

Event route
In making his recommendations, Graham consulted with other staff to obtain information. He cross-referenced to the evidence used in PC (a). In addition, Graham obtained information about current best practice for induction programmes from a professional management institute to which he was affiliated. This was also used as evidence.

Event route
Emma was also able to cross-reference to the evidence used for PC (a), where she obtained information from staff and other managers. She also included computerised printouts detailing current shift patterns, timescales for production of particular components and break times, which she used to calculate timescales and human resource requirements for the night shift. These were also submitted as evidence and clearly explained and justified in Emma's analysis.

Ideas for evidence

▌ Examples of information used to inform recommendations.

▌ Statistics.

▌ National legislation.

▌ Internal information.

▌ The views of relevant people.

▌ Media information.

▌ Personal report explaining the sufficiency, validity and reliability of the information.

Your ideas for evidence

Description of evidence	Location of evidence	Opportunities for cross-referencing	Reflection and analysis

K&U links

Suggested reading for knowledge and understanding purposes:

Cole, G.A., *Management: Theory and Practice*, 5th edition, chapters 19, 21 and 26.

Mullins, L.J., *Management and Organisational Behaviour*, 4th edition, chapters 7, 9 and 13.

Needham, D. et al., *Business for Higher Awards*, chapters 9, 10, 11 and 27.

Cross-referencing

Evidence and knowledge from this element can be used in the following mandatory units of NVQ Management Level 3: **B1**, **C4**, **D1**; and the following optional units: **C9**, **C12**, **C15**, **E5**, **E8**, **F5**.

Element A1.3	# Make recommendations for improvements to work activities

Performance Criterion

(c) Your recommendations for improvements are consistent with the objectives of your team and organisation.

> Link to previous evidence used throughout this unit, if appropriate. Explain how you take team and organisational objectives into account when making recommendations for improvements to work activities. Detail your recommendations and demonstrate how they support or complement existing objectives.

Interpretation

◼ What are the relevant team and organisational objectives?

◼ How do they inform your recommendations for improvements to work activities?

◼ How do your recommendations support or complement objectives?

Candidate illustration

Event route
Graham highlighted the recommendations made in his report concerning improvements to the local induction process. In a personal report he detailed his organisation's involvement with the Investors in People (IIP) award, explaining that the recommendations supported the principles of IIP and therefore supported its achievement.

Event route
Emma highlighted her original brief as evidence, explaining the need to extend production capacity in line with seasonal demand for products. She obtained a witness testimony from her line manager confirming that her recommendations supported local and organisational objectives.

Ideas for evidence

◼ Examples of recommendations that you have made.

◼ Details of team and organisational objectives.

◼ Personal report detailing the contribution made by your recommendations to the achievement of the objectives.

◼ Witness testimony from senior personnel confirming this.

Your ideas for evidence

Description of evidence	Location of evidence	Opportunities for cross-referencing	Reflection and analysis

K&U links

Suggested reading for knowledge and understanding purposes:

Cole, G.A., *Management: Theory and Practice*, 5th edition, chapters 19, 21 and 26.

Mullins, L.J., *Management and Organisational Behaviour*, 4th edition, chapters 7, 9 and 13.

Needham, D. et al., *Business for Higher Awards*, chapters 9, 10, 11 and 27.

Cross-referencing

Evidence and knowledge from this element can be used in the following mandatory units of NVQ Management Level 3: **B1**, **C4**, **D1**; and the following optional units: **C9**, **C12**, **C15**, **E5**, **E8**, **F5**.

Element A1.3 Make recommendations for improvements to work activities

Performance Criterion

(d) Your recommendations take into account the impact of introducing changes on other parts of your organisation.

> This performance criterion requires you to highlight any implications that your recommendations have for other parts of your organisation and explain how these implications have informed your recommendations.

Interpretation

■ Do you consider the implications of your recommendations for other areas of the organisation?

■ How do you incorporate these implications into your final recommendations?

Candidate illustration

Event route
Graham cross-referenced to the recommendations made in his final report (see PC (c)), which highlighted the likely impact of their introduction. The conclusions of the report were also evidenced as they included analyses of induction processes, the increased responsibility of senior staff and management, support and resources needed from the internal training department, and the likely timescales involved.

Event route
Emma cross-referenced to the evidence used for PC (a), where she consulted with managers and supervisors from other teams and departments. One of the purposes of these meetings was to identify the likely impact of the proposed night shift on other areas of the organisation (for example security and the canteen). The relevant parts of the minutes were annotated and Emma clearly explained her actions in her analysis.

Ideas for evidence

■ Cross-reference to existing evidence, if appropriate.

■ Details of the recommendations made.

■ Details of methods of making recommendations:
  – presentations;
  – reports;
  – meetings.

■ Personal statement detailing the other people involved.

Your ideas for evidence

Description of evidence	Location of evidence	Opportunities for cross-referencing	Reflection and analysis

K&U links

Suggested reading for knowledge and understanding purposes:

Cole, G.A., *Management: Theory and Practice*, 5th edition, chapters 19, 21 and 26.

Mullins, L.J., *Management and Organisational Behaviour*, 4th edition, chapters 7, 9 and 13.

Needham, D. et al., *Business for Higher Awards*, chapters 9, 10, 11 and 27.

Cross-referencing

Evidence and knowledge from this element can be used in the following mandatory units of NVQ Management Level 3: **B1, C4, D1**; and the following optional units: **C9, C12, C15, E5, E8, F5**.

Element A1.3 | Make recommendations for improvements to work activities

Performance Criterion

(e) You make recommendations promptly to the relevant people.

> You should link to previous evidence used in this element, if appropriate. Explain the timescales involved in making your recommendations and detail their significance. Highlight who the relevant people were. They should include team members, peers, higher-level managers, or sponsors and specialists.

Interpretation

- What were the timescales involved in making your recommendations?
- How were they made?
- Who else was involved?

Candidate illustration

Event route
Graham referenced the recommendations section of his report (see PC (c)) and explained the report format. He also included the overhead transparencies and handouts used in a briefing seminar he had given for managers. In his analysis, Graham detailed the people who attended, highlighting their responsibilities for induction.

Event route
Emma submitted her final report, together with recommendations, to the project board. She held a meeting with them to answer questions and discuss issues relating to the night shift. The project report and minutes of the meeting were submitted as evidence. In a personal statement, Emma identified the members of the project board, explaining their responsibilities and why they were involved.

Your ideas for evidence

Description of evidence	Location of evidence	Opportunities for cross-referencing	Reflection and analysis

K&U links

Suggested reading for knowledge and understanding purposes:

Cole, G.A., *Management: Theory and Practice*, 5th edition, chapters 19, 21 and 26.

Mullins, L.J., *Management and Organisational Behaviour*, 4th edition, chapters 7, 9 and 13.

Needham, D. et al., *Business for Higher Awards*, chapters 10, 11 and 27.

Cross-referencing

Evidence and knowledge from this element can be used in the following mandatory units of NVQ Management Level 3: **B1**, **C4**, **D1**; and the following optional units: **C9**, **C12**, **C15**, **E5**, **E8**, **F5**.

| *Element A1.3* | # Make recommendations for improvements to work activities |

Performance Criterion

(f) *You make recommendations in a manner and form consistent with your organisation's procedures.*

> Link to evidence previously used in this element, if appropriate.
> Explain the way in which you have presented your recommendations.
> Detail any organisational procedures that you have followed.

Interpretation

■ How are recommendations made?

■ Does the nature of the recommendations inform the manner of the presentation?

■ Which organisational procedures inform the making of recommendations?

Candidate illustration

Event route
Both Graham and Emma were able to cross-reference to their reports. Each explained the report format in their analyses, detailing the 'house style' required.

Ideas for evidence

■ Cross-reference to existing evidence used in this element, if appropriate.

■ Examples of recommendations.

■ Explanation of the format used for presentations.

■ Details of any relevant organisational procedures and how they have informed your presentation of recommendations.

Your ideas for evidence

Description of evidence	Location of evidence	Opportunities for cross-referencing	Reflection and analysis

K&U links

Suggested reading for knowledge and understanding purposes:

Cole, G.A., *Management: Theory and Practice,* 5th edition, chapters 19, 21 and 26.

Mullins, L.J., *Management and Organisational Behaviour,* 4th edition, chapters 7, 9 and 13.

Needham, D. et al., *Business for Higher Awards,* chapters 10, 11 and 14.

Cross-referencing

Evidence and knowledge from this element can be used in the following mandatory units of NVQ Management Level 3: **B1, C4, D1**; and the following optional units: **C9, C12, C15, E5, E8, F5**.

CHAPTER 5

Unit B1

Support the efficient use of resources

Element B1.1   Make recommendations for the use of resources

Performance Criterion

(a) *You give relevant people the opportunity to provide information on the resources your team needs.*

> You should explain how you provide these kinds of opportunities. Detail how and what information has been provided by relevant people. Relevant people should include at least two of the following throughout this element: team members, peers, higher-level managers or sponsors.

Interpretation

▌ What kinds of information regarding resource needs do you use?

▌ How is it obtained?

▌ Who is this information obtained from?

▌ How are opportunities for providing this information given?

Candidate illustration

Event route

Graham focused on a specific project in which his team was involved. It concerned measuring the costs of the contracted supply of fresh foods to the unit (currently supplied by the council's central purchasing division) against the costs of changing to a system of purchasing locally from town retailers (i.e., autonomously). The council was contemplating reducing the responsibilities of the central purchasing unit in order to reduce administrative costs. The team's remit was to estimate the costs, both financial and in terms of staff time, associated with the proposed scheme. Graham called a team meeting in order to introduce the project and to seek estimates from team members of the amount of time they would need to purchase fresh provisions locally. Graham included the minutes of the meeting as evidence, and clearly explained the project brief in his analysis.

Event route

Emma was able to continue her focus on the feasibility study she had undertaken regarding the introduction of a night shift (see Unit A1, Element A1.3, PC (a)). During her preparation for the study, Emma consulted members of the two teams to identify issues surrounding the support services night-time staff would require: breaks, canteen services, security concerns and work times. These were noted during meetings with staff and collated for the purpose of the final report. Emma submitted her notes from the meetings with staff, together with a highlighted section from the final feasibility report detailing anticipated resource requirements.

Ideas for evidence

▌ Cross-reference to evidence used in the previous unit, if appropriate.

▌ Minutes of consultative meetings held with your team.

▪ Notes of conversations held with team members.

▪ Supervision notes.

▪ Extracts from reports that detail feedback from the team concerning the use of resources.

Your ideas for evidence

Description of evidence	Location of evidence	Opportunities for cross-referencing	Reflection and analysis

K&U links

Suggested reading for knowledge and understanding purposes:

Cole, G.A., *Management: Theory and Practice,* 5th edition, chapters 6, 19, 23 and 26.

Mullins, L.J., *Management and Organisational Behaviour,* 4th edition, chapter 7.

Needham, D. et al., *Business for Higher Awards,* chapters 8, 9, 10, 11, 14 and 27.

Cross-referencing

Evidence and knowledge from this element can be used in the following mandatory units of NVQ Management Level 3: **A1, C4, D1**; and the following optional units: **C9, C12, E5, E8, F5**.

<table>
<tr><td>Element B1.1</td><td># Make recommendations for the use of resources</td></tr>
</table>

Element B1.1 Make recommendations for the use of resources

Performance Criterion

(b) Your recommendations for the use of resources take account of relevant past experience.

> Detail specific recommendations that you have made. Throughout this element, you should include evidence of both your short-term and long-term recommendations. Explain how historical information and previous experience informed these recommendations.

Interpretation

▪ What kinds of recommendations regarding the use of resources have you made?

▪ How have your recommendations been informed by your previous experience and that of others?

Candidate illustration

Event route
Graham highlighted parts of his final report on the local purchasing project (see PC (a)), which gave a historical background to purchasing procedures, based on his and others' experiences.

Event route
Emma also highlighted extracts from her report on the introduction of a night shift (see PC (a)). The extracts related to anticipated shift patterns in terms of tea and meal breaks, which were based on her and her staff's experiences of working the two existing day shifts.

Ideas for evidence

▪ Cross-reference to existing evidence used for this element, if appropriate.

▪ Extracts from reports.

▪ Forecasts based on previous experience.

▪ Personal statement detailing use of previous experience.

Your ideas for evidence

Description of evidence	Location of evidence	Opportunities for cross-referencing	Reflection and analysis

K&U links

Suggested reading for knowledge and understanding purposes:

Cole, G.A., *Management: Theory and Practice*, 5th edition, chapters 6, 19, 23 and 26.

Needham, D. et al., *Business for Higher Awards*, chapters 8, 9, 10, 11 and 27.

Cross-referencing

Evidence and knowledge from this element can be used in the following mandatory units of NVQ Management Level 3: **A1, C4, D1**; and the following optional units: **C9, C12, E5, E8, F5**.

Element B1.1   Make recommendations for the use of resources

Performance Criterion

(c) Your recommendations take account of trends and developments which are likely to affect the use of resources.

You should link to previous evidence used in this element, if relevant. Explain any trends and developments that have informed your recommendations. Highlight why they were significant and the likely effect they would have on the use of resources.

Interpretation

▪ What kinds of recommendations have you made?

▪ How were they informed by trends and developments?

▪ What were the implications for resource usage?

Candidate illustration

Event route
Graham again drew evidence from his project report on localised purchasing for fresh foods. He highlighted the section on the seasonal availability and consequent price fluctuations of some fresh produce, particularly fruit and vegetables. It was found that price fluctuations and availability were considerably more acute when using the localised system.

Event route
Emma continued to focus on her night shift feasibility study. In costing the shift, she sought advice from senior management regarding its duration throughout the year. As the night shift was to be used only to meet increased demand, she needed to know when demand rose and fell in order to cost the shift accurately. As evidence, Emma included her memo requesting the information, the reply she received, and evidence that she incorporated the information into the final report.

Ideas for evidence

▪ Link to previous evidence used in this and other elements, if appropriate.

▪ Extracts from reports highlighting trends and developments that affect resource use.

▪ Memos requesting information on trends and developments.

▪ Replies to your requests.

Your ideas for evidence

Description of evidence	Location of evidence	Opportunities for cross-referencing	Reflection and analysis

K&U links

Suggested reading for knowledge and understanding purposes:

Cole, G.A., *Management: Theory and Practice*, 5th edition, chapters 6, 19, 23 and 26.

Needham, D. et al., *Business for Higher Awards*, chapters 8, 9, 10, 11 and 27.

Cross-referencing

Evidence and knowledge from this element can be used in the following mandatory units of NVQ Management Level 3: **A1, C4, D1**; and the following optional units: **C9, C12, E5, E8, F5**.

<table>
<tr><td>

Element **B1.1**

</td><td>

Make recommendations for the use of resources

</td></tr>
</table>

Performance Criterion

(d) Your recommendations are consistent with team objectives and organisational policies.

> Link to previous evidence used in this element, if appropriate. Using specific recommendations for the use of resources, highlight how they have complemented or supported objectives and policies. Explain the significance of your recommendations in relation to the relevant objectives and policies.

Interpretation

▪ What kinds of recommendations have you made?

▪ How were they informed by objectives and policies?

▪ What were the implications for resource usage?

Candidate illustration

Event route
Graham submitted as evidence the initial request for the project, received from senior management, and his written report, together with recommendations made. He explained that the project was undertaken by the company to maximise the quality of services provided and to ensure the efficient and effective use of both financial and physical resources. As supporting evidence, Graham obtained a witness testimony from his line manager confirming his evidence and analysis.

Event route
Emma highlighted the recommendations made regarding the night shift feasibility study. In a personal statement she detailed each recommendation and explained how it supported the organisation's requirements regarding the night shift. She also detailed how the recommendations had taken into account her production team's views and objectives for the future.

Ideas for evidence

▪ Link to previous evidence used in this and other elements, if appropriate.

▪ Examples of recommendations used.

▪ Details of team objectives and organisational policies and their significance.

▪ Personal statement explaining your recommendations.

Your ideas for evidence

Description of evidence	Location of evidence	Opportunities for cross-referencing	Reflection and analysis

K&U links

Suggested reading for knowledge and understanding purposes:

Cole, G.A., *Management: Theory and Practice,* 5th edition, chapters 6, 19, 23 and 26.

Needham, D. et al., *Business for Higher Awards,* chapters 8, 9, 10, 11 and 27.

Cross-referencing

Evidence and knowledge from this element can be used in the following mandatory units of NVQ Management Level 3: **A1, C4, D1;** and the following optional units: **C9, C12, E5, E8, F5.**

Element B1.1 Make recommendations for the use of resources

Performance Criterion

(e) Your recommendations clearly indicate the potential benefits you expect from the planned use of resources.

> Link to previous evidence used in this element, if appropriate. Explain the significance of your recommendations and justify how they will improve the use of resources.

Interpretation

- ■ How are the benefits of your recommendations indicated?
- ■ What are the benefits for resource usage?

Candidate illustration

Event route
Graham cross-referenced to the findings and recommendations sections of his report on centralised and localised purchasing. In the findings he had explained that purchasing locally involved significant increases in expenditure of both time and money. This was used as the justification for his recommendations to continue with the centralised purchasing system.

Event route
Emma undertook a cost–benefit analysis for the night shift, based on additional variable costs incurred and the increase in production assuming full capacity was maintained. She highlighted this part of her feasibility study and explained it fully in her analysis. The study informed her recommendations that the night shift was viable and it would indeed increase production levels in line with anticipated demand.

Ideas for evidence

- ■ Link to previous evidence used in this and other elements, if appropriate.
- ■ Examples of recommendations made.
- ■ Extracts from reports detailing the benefits of your recommendations regarding resource usage.
- ■ Personal statement explaining your actions.

Your ideas for evidence

Description of evidence	Location of evidence	Opportunities for cross-referencing	Reflection and analysis

K&U links   Suggested reading for knowledge and understanding purposes:

Cole, G.A., *Management: Theory and Practice,* 5th edition, chapters 6, 19, 23 and 26.

Needham, D. et al., *Business for Higher Awards,* chapters 8, 9, 10, 11 and 27.

Cross-referencing   Evidence and knowledge from this element can be used in the following mandatory units of NVQ Management Level 3: **A1, C4, D1**; and the following optional units: **C9, C12, E5, E8, F5**.

Make recommendations for the use of resources

Performance Criterion

(f) *Your recommendations are presented to relevant people in an appropriate and timely manner.*

> Link to previous evidence used in this element, if appropriate. Explain your methods of presentation and detail who the relevant people are. Highlight the timescales involved and their significance.

Interpretation

◼ How are your recommendations presented?

◼ Who are they being presented to?

◼ What are the timescales involved?

Candidate illustration

Event route
Graham reported to a project board and detailed who they were in a personal statement. He also cross-referenced to his original project brief (see PC (d)), which detailed the timescales required. He obtained a witness testimony from one of the board confirming that he and his team kept to all deadlines.

Event route
Emma cross-referenced to Unit A1, Element A1.3, PC (e), where she identified the people who received her final report on the introduction of the night shift. She also included a testimony from her line manager confirming that a full report had been requested and that Emma's report complied with the 'house style' required.

Ideas for evidence

◼ Cross-reference to existing evidence used in this and other elements, if appropriate.

◼ Details of the people in receipt of your recommendations.

◼ Project briefs detailing requirements.

◼ Examples of recommendations and justification for the presentation style used.

Your ideas for evidence

Description of evidence	Location of evidence	Opportunities for cross-referencing	Reflection and analysis

K&U links

Suggested reading for knowledge and understanding purposes:

Cole, G.A., *Management: Theory and Practice,* 5th edition, chapters 6, 19, 23 and 26.

Needham, D. et al., *Business for Higher Awards,* chapters 8, 9, 10, 11, 14 and 27.

Cross-referencing

Evidence and knowledge from this element can be used in the following mandatory units of NVQ Management Level 3: **A1, C4, D1**; and the following optional units: **C9, C12, E5, E8, F5**.

| Element B1.2 | **Contribute to the control of resources** |

Performance Criterion

(a) *You give relevant people opportunities to take individual responsibility for the efficient use of resources.*

> Explain your span of control and the resources for which you are responsible. Detail instances where you have temporarily or permanently delegated responsibility for use of these resources to team members or peers.

Interpretation

■ Which resources are you responsible for?

■ How do you give others responsibility for the use of these resources?

Candidate illustration

Event route
Graham submitted two separate supervision documents relating to members of his team. He highlighted the sections detailing their responsibilities for monitoring the distribution of drugs and medication and the inspection of incoming goods. In his analysis, he explained the decision to delegate responsibility for these areas.

Event route
Emma detailed a series of meetings held with the other team leader in her production area. Minutes of the meetings were included which showed how both team leaders coordinated shifts to ensure cover at all times. The minutes also showed their respective responsibilities for monitoring the production process.

Ideas for evidence

■ Supervision documentation.

■ Minutes of team meetings.

■ Minutes of meetings with colleagues and peers to discuss responsibilities.

■ Personal statement explaining your actions.

Your ideas for evidence

Description of evidence	Location of evidence	Opportunities for cross-referencing	Reflection and analysis

K&U links   Suggested reading for knowledge and understanding purposes:

Cole, G.A., *Management: Theory and Practice,* 5th edition, chapters 26, 28 and 29.

Mullins, L.J., *Management and Organisational Behaviour,* 4th edition, chapter 16.

Needham, D. et al., *Business for Higher Awards,* chapters 8, 9, 10, 11, 14 and 27.

Cross-referencing   Evidence and knowledge from this element can be used in the following mandatory units of NVQ Management Level 3: **A1, C1, C4, D1**; and the following optional units: **C9, C12, C15, E5, E8, F5, F7**.

Element B1.2 Contribute to the control of resources

Performance Criterion

(b) *You monitor the use of resources under your control at appropriate intervals.*

> You should give specific examples of the monitoring process you use or are involved in. Explain how monitoring works and the significance of the timescales involved.

Interpretation

■ How is the use of the resources for which you are responsible monitored?

■ What is your contribution to the monitoring?

■ What are the timescales involved?

■ How are they significant?

Candidate illustration

Event route
As part of his company's quality management system, Graham's responsibility is to monitor aspects of the unit's operation, including the use of drugs and medication, equipment and food supplies. The company had developed a series of pro-formas designed to monitor all areas, and Graham had to complete them every month. A range of these completed quality documents were submitted as evidence.

Event route
Emma was able to cross-reference to Unit A1, Element A1.1, PC (d), where she included printouts comparing forecast and actual production statistics. Emma's responsibility was to monitor components and work rates and explain any variances in the statistics. She included a personal report detailing her responsibilities and actions concerning resource usage.

Ideas for evidence

■ Completed monitoring documentation.

■ Statistical information.

■ Details of timescales involved.

■ Reports concerning monitoring of resource usage.

Your ideas for evidence

Description of evidence	Location of evidence	Opportunities for cross-referencing	Reflection and analysis

K&U links

Suggested reading for knowledge and understanding purposes:

Cole, G.A., *Management: Theory and Practice*, 5th edition, chapters 26, 28 and 29.

Mullins, L.J., *Management and Organisational Behaviour*, 4th edition, chapter 17.

Needham, D. et al., *Business for Higher Awards*, chapters 8, 9, 10, 11, 14 and 27.

Cross-referencing

Evidence and knowledge from this element can be used in the following mandatory units of NVQ Management Level 3: **A1, C1, C4, D1**; and the following optional units: **C9, C12, C15, E5, E8, F5, F7**.

Element B1.2   Contribute to the control of resources

Performance Criterion

(c) *The use of resources by your team is efficient and takes into account the potential impact on the environment.*

> Link to PC (b), if appropriate. Explain the outcomes of monitoring resource usage. Detail how you ensure efficiency and take environmental issues into consideration.

Interpretation

■ How do you ensure the efficient use of resources?

■ What are the potential positive or negative implications for the environment as a result of the use of particular resources?

Candidate illustration

Event route
Graham focused on food supplies for this performance criterion. He included documentation measuring waste, which was used to identify popular (and unpopular) dishes and quantities for ordering. In his analysis, Graham detailed his knowledge of the environmental implications (in terms of waste management) of the work for which he was responsible.

Event route
Emma cross-referenced to the statistics evidenced in support of PC (b), which showed forecasted against actual production figures. These figures demonstrated that her team achieved targets and she explained their implications in her analysis. In addition, Emma submitted monitoring documents detailing the number of faulty components received from suppliers. Emma explained in her analysis that company policy was to return these to the supplier for environmental reasons. Emma's assessor felt that her evidence was not sufficient to meet the requirements of this PC. She asked Emma to provide evidence of the company policy referred to and to explain why faulty components were returned to suppliers. Emma re-submitted this additional evidence, with a letter from her supplier explaining that faulty components were recycled, in the interests of the environment.

Ideas for evidence

■ Documentation stating efficient use of resources:
  – statistics;
  – monitoring of faulty components or equipment;
  – monitoring of wastage.

■ Details of your or your organisation's environmental policy and how you comply with it.

Your ideas for evidence

Description of evidence	Location of evidence	Opportunities for cross-referencing	Reflection and analysis

K&U links

Suggested reading for knowledge and understanding purposes:

Cole, G.A., *Management: Theory and Practice,* 5th edition, chapters 26, 28 and 29.

Mullins, L.J., *Management and Organisational Behaviour,* 4th edition, chapter 17.

Needham, D. et al., *Business for Higher Awards,* chapters 8, 9, 10, 11 and 27.

Cross-referencing

Evidence and knowledge from this element can be used in the following mandatory units of NVQ Management Level 3: **A1, C1, C4, D1**; and the following optional units: **C9, C12, C15, E5, E8, F5, F7**.

Element **B1.2**   Contribute to the control of resources

Performance Criterion

(d) You monitor the quality of resources continuously and ensure consistency in product and service delivery.

> Detail how resources are monitored for quality and how you ensure that they meet the specifications or requirements of your organisation. Explain how the quality of resources affects the consistency of the products or services for which you are responsible.

Interpretation

◼ How are resources monitored for quality?

◼ What specifications or requirements are they monitored against?

◼ How do you ensure consistency of the products or services for which you are responsible?

Candidate illustration

Event route
Both Graham and Emma were able to cross-reference to evidence used in PCs (a), (b) and (c) of this element. In their analyses, they detailed the significance of the timescales involved and the contribution made by the various kinds of monitoring to delivering a consistently high standard of products and services.

Ideas for evidence

◼ Cross-reference to existing evidence used in this element, if appropriate.

◼ Monitoring documentation.

◼ Statistical information.

◼ Details of the timescales involved.

◼ Personal statement explaining the importance of consistency in the delivery of products and services.

Your ideas for evidence

Description of evidence	Location of evidence	Opportunities for cross-referencing	Reflection and analysis

K&U links

Suggested reading for knowledge and understanding purposes:

Cole, G.A., *Management: Theory and Practice*, 5th edition, chapters 26, 28 and 29.

Mullins, L.J., *Management and Organisational Behaviour*, 4th edition, chapter 7.

Needham, D. et al., *Business for Higher Awards*, chapters 8, 9, 10, 11 and 27.

Cross-referencing

Evidence and knowledge from this element can be used in the following mandatory units of NVQ Management Level 3: **A1, C1, C4, D1**; and the following optional units: **C9, C12, C15, E5, E8, F5, F7**.

Element B1.2 Contribute to the control of resources

Performance Criterion

(e) You identify problems with resources promptly, and make recommendations for corrective action to the relevant people as soon as possible.

> To meet the requirements of this PC you will have to detail specific instances where your monitoring has identified defective or unacceptable resources. Explain the problem and the action that was taken to rectify it. Corrective action should include at least two of the following: altering activities, modifying the use of resources and renegotiating allocation of resources. Relevant people should include team members or peers.

Interpretation

- How do you identify problems with resources?
- What are the causes of these problems?
- What action have you recommended should be taken?
- To whom were recommendations made?

Candidate illustration

Event route

Graham focused on a specific instance where a member of his staff identified a discrepancy in a delivery of fresh food supplies (see Element B1.1, PC (a)). The quantity of vegetables ordered did not match that supplied. Graham took action by contacting the supplier and requesting delivery of the outstanding quantity. He explained his actions and those of his team members, and submitted as evidence a copy of the order and delivery notes highlighting the discrepancy.

Event route

Emma also focused on a specific instance where a new component supplier had been given a trial contract. She monitored faulty components over time and found that there were more faults with the new components. As evidence she highlighted the contract with the new supplier, monitoring documentation and a written memo to the production manager recommending that the contract be terminated.

Ideas for evidence

- Details of specific problems with resources.
- Documentation relating to the nature of the problem:
  – invoices and delivery notes;
  – monitoring documentation.
- Memos making recommendations.
- Witness testimony from others involved confirming your actions.

Your ideas for evidence

Description of evidence	Location of evidence	Opportunities for cross-referencing	Reflection and analysis

K&U links

Suggested reading for knowledge and understanding purposes:

Cole, G.A., *Management: Theory and Practice,* 5th edition, chapters 26, 28 and 29.

Mullins, L.J., *Management and Organisational Behaviour,* 4th edition, chapter 11.

Needham, D. et al., *Business for Higher Awards,* chapters 8, 9, 10, 11, 14 and 27.

Cross-referencing

Evidence and knowledge from this element can be used in the following mandatory units of NVQ Management Level 3: **A1, C1, C4, D1**; and the following optional units: **C9, C12, C15, E5, E8, F5, F7**.

Element B1.2 Contribute to the control of resources

Performance Criterion

(f) *You make recommendations for improving the use of resources to relevant people in an appropriate and timely manner.*

> You should give examples of general or specific recommendations for improvements that you have made. Explain the circumstances and the involvement of other people. Detail the timescales involved and your approach to making the recommendations.

Interpretation

◼ In what circumstances have you made recommendations for improving the use of resources?

◼ Who else was involved?

◼ To whom were the recommendations made?

◼ How were the recommendations made?

◼ What were the timescales involved?

Candidate illustration

Event route
Graham cross-referenced to PC (c) of this element, where he used documentation to record food waste. As a result of this monitoring, Graham found that particular foods were not being consumed, particularly vegetables. Graham recommended to the unit manager that monitoring should continue following a reduction in the amounts of fresh vegetables ordered. As additional evidence, Graham submitted the memo to his manager making the recommendation and explained the timescales involved in his analysis.

Event route
Emma cross-referenced to the feasibility study she had undertaken regarding the introduction of a night shift (see Unit A1 and Element B1.1, PC (a)). She referenced her final report and highlighted the recommendations section. She also cross-referenced to Element B1.1, PC (f), where she had submitted a testimony from her line manager confirming the appropriateness of her report format.

Ideas for evidence

◼ Cross-reference to existing evidence for this and other elements, if appropriate.

◼ Details of recommendations made:
   – letters;
   – email;
   – memos;
   – reports.

◼ Witness testimony from others involved confirming your methods of making recommendations.

◼ Details of the significance of the timescales involved.

Your ideas for evidence

Description of evidence	Location of evidence	Opportunities for cross-referencing	Reflection and analysis

K&U links

Suggested reading for knowledge and understanding purposes:

Cole, G.A., *Management: Theory and Practice*, 5th edition, chapters 26, 28 and 29.

Needham, D. et al., *Business for Higher Awards*, chapters 8, 9, 10, 11, 14 and 27.

Cross-referencing

Evidence and knowledge from this element can be used in the following mandatory units of NVQ Management Level 3: **A1**, **C1**, **C4**, **D1**; and the following optional units: **C9**, **C12**, **C15**, **E5**, **E8**, **F5**, **F7**.

Element B1.2 Contribute to the control of resources

Performance Criterion

(g) Your records relating to the use of resources are complete, accurate and available to authorised people only.

> If you can, provide examples of the records that you keep. Explain how they are used and why accuracy is important. Detail the storage, retrieval and confidentiality systems that are operated. If, for reasons of security or confidentiality, you cannot include copies of these records, arrange an observational assessment (see pages 19 and 22) with your assessor.

Interpretation

- What kinds of records relating to the use of resources are kept?
- How do you ensure that they are maintained correctly?
- How are they stored?
- How are they accessed?
- Is confidentiality an issue?

Candidate illustration

Event route

Both Graham and Emma cross-referenced to the variety of monitoring records submitted throughout this element (see PCs (a), (b) and (c)). In their analyses, they detailed the importance of accuracy and explained the storage and retrieval systems in place. Graham obtained a testimony from his line manager confirming the accuracy of his records and storage systems. Emma invited her NVQ assessor to observe records and storage and retrieval systems in her factory.

Ideas for evidence

- Cross-reference to existing evidence used in this element, if appropriate.
- Examples of complete and accurate records and documentation relating to the use of resources.
- Details of storage and retrieval and confidentiality systems.
- Witness testimony from others involved.
- Records of observational assessment in the workplace.

Your ideas for evidence

Description of evidence	Location of evidence	Opportunities for cross-referencing	Reflection and analysis

K&U links

Suggested reading for knowledge and understanding purposes:

Cole, G.A., *Management: Theory and Practice,* 5th edition, chapters 26, 28 and 29.

Mullins, L.J., *Management and Organisational Behaviour,* 4th edition, chapter 17.

Needham, D. et al., *Business for Higher Awards,* chapters 8, 9, 10, 11, 14, 25 and 27.

Cross-referencing

Evidence and knowledge from this element can be used in the following mandatory units of NVQ Management Level 3: **A1, C1, C4, D1**; and the following optional units: **C9, C12, C15, E5, E8, F5, F7**.

CHAPTER 6

Unit C1

Manage yourself

Element C1.1 Develop your own skills to improve your performance

Performance Criterion

(a) *You assess your skills and identify your development needs at appropriate intervals.*

> You should focus on specific instances where you have undertaken a personal review of your training and development needs. Explain the process and the significance of the timescales involved.

Interpretation

- How do you assess your own training and development needs?
- What are the timescales involved?
- Why are these appropriate?

Candidate illustration

Event route
Throughout this element, Graham focused on his supervision sessions with his line manager and their links to his personal development. For this performance criterion, Graham submitted photocopied diary extracts showing scheduled supervision sessions with his manager. In addition, he submitted copies of three personal supervision documents showing that he had assessed his skills and development needs, in discussion with his manager, over a period of time.

Event route
Emma submitted extracts from her personal development portfolio (PDP), which showed how she had developed her time management and communication skills over the previous year. The portfolio was regularly reviewed with the company training officer. Emma obtained a testimony from the training officer confirming her development.

Ideas for evidence

- Diary extracts showing meetings relating to personal development.
- Personal supervision documents.
- Extracts from personal development portfolios (PDPs).
- Details of the significance of the timescales involved.

Your ideas for evidence

Description of evidence	Location of evidence	Opportunities for cross-referencing	Reflection and analysis

K&U links

Suggested reading for knowledge and understanding purposes:

Cole, G.A., *Management: Theory and Practice,* 5th edition, chapters 27 and 44.

Mullins, L.J., *Management and Organisational Behaviour,* 4th edition, chapters 4 and 15.

Needham, D. et al., *Business for Higher Awards,* chapters 10 and 25.

Cross-referencing

Evidence and knowledge from this element can be used in the following mandatory units of NVQ Management Level 3: **A1, C4**; and the following optional unit: **C9.**

| *Element C1.1* | # Develop your own skills to improve your performance |

Performance Criterion

(b) *Your assessment takes account of the skills you need to work effectively with other team members.*

> You will need to detail any stages in your personal training and development needs analysis that focus on team work. Throughout the element, your assessments must take account of work objectives, personal objectives, and organisational policies and requirements.

Interpretation

▪ Do team-working skills form part of your personal development assessment?

▪ What are the skills needed?

▪ How are assessments recorded?

Candidate illustration

Event route
Graham cross-referenced to the supervision documents used in PC (a) of this element. He highlighted notes of conversations with his line manager about the possibility of his providing cascade training on team building to his staff. In other words, it was planned for Graham to attend a course on team building, and he would feedback information to his team members by arranging and delivering a training session for them. In this way, both he and his team would benefit.

Event route
Emma continued to use extracts from her personal development portfolio, which detailed her attendance of an assertiveness training course following a personal training needs analysis (TNA). The TNA documentation was also included as evidence.

Ideas for evidence

▪ Personal supervision documents.

▪ Extracts from personal development portfolios (PDPs).

▪ Training needs analysis (TNA) documentation.

Your ideas for evidence

Description of evidence	Location of evidence	Opportunities for cross-referencing	Reflection and analysis

K&U links

Suggested reading for knowledge and understanding purposes:

Cole, G.A., *Management: Theory and Practice*, 5th edition, chapters 27 and 44.

Mullins, L.J., *Management and Organisational Behaviour*, 4th edition, chapters 4 and 15.

Needham, D. et al., *Business for Higher Awards*, chapters 10 and 25.

Cross-referencing

Evidence and knowledge from this element can be used in the following mandatory units of NVQ Management Level 3: **A1**, **C4**; and the following optional unit: **C9**.

Element C1.1 Develop your own skills to improve your performance

Performance Criterion

(c) *Your plans for developing your skills are consistent with the needs you have identified.*

> You should include examples of your personal development plans (or equivalent) and highlight how the plans are designed to meet your development needs. Focus on what the plan contains and explain how this will help you to develop the skills identified in your assessment.

Interpretation

▪ Do you have personal development plans or equivalents?

▪ How do they support your development needs?

Candidate illustration

Event route

Graham cross-referenced to the evidence used for PC (b) of this element. In his analysis, he explained that he had identified a skills requirement relating to motivating his team. Graham explained that the team-building event identified as appropriate was designed to address this.

Event route

Emma also cross-referenced to the evidence used for PC (b) of this element. She explained that the training needs analysis (TNA) process assisted her in identifying a gap in her skills relating to time management. Emma explained in her analysis that the planned event, a time management course, was designed to assist managers to delegate effectively without using coercion or aggressive language and to focus on process issues rather than tasks.

Ideas for evidence

▪ Cross-reference to evidence previously used in this element, if appropriate.

▪ Personal supervision documents.

▪ Extracts from personal development plans.

▪ Completed appraisal documentation.

▪ Completed training needs analysis (TNA) documentation.

Your ideas for evidence

Description of evidence	Location of evidence	Opportunities for cross-referencing	Reflection and analysis

K&U links

Suggested reading for knowledge and understanding purposes:

Cole, G.A., *Management: Theory and Practice,* 5th edition, chapters 27 and 44.

Mullins, L.J., *Management and Organisational Behaviour,* 4th edition, chapters 4 and 15.

Needham, D. et al., *Business for Higher Awards,* chapters 10 and 25.

Cross-referencing

Evidence and knowledge from this element can be used in the following mandatory units of NVQ Management Level 3: **A1**, **C4**; and the following optional unit: **C9**.

Element C1.1	# Develop your own skills to improve your performance

Performance Criterion

(d) *Your plans for developing your skills contain specific, measurable and realistic objectives.*

> You can link to evidence used in PC (c), if appropriate. Include examples of your personal development plan (or equivalent), detailing in your analysis how you ensure that your objectives are achievable. Explain how the objectives are linked to the skills that you need to develop.

Interpretation

■ How are objectives identified in your personal development plan?

■ Are they achievable?

■ Are they clear?

■ How will you measure your achievement?

Candidate illustration

Event route
Graham was again able to highlight sections of his supervision documents (see PC (a)), detailing the area in need of development, the planned method of personal development, the desired outcome of the development, timescales and review dates relating to the team-building training for managers and their staff.

Event route
Emma cross-referenced to her personal development portfolio, where she had set personal objectives relating to putting training into practice. She highlighted the relevant sections and gave a detailed account of her objectives in the analysis of evidence.

Ideas for evidence

■ Cross-reference to evidence previously used in this element, if appropriate.

■ Personal supervision documents.

■ Extracts from personal development plans.

■ Completed appraisal documentation.

■ Completed training needs analysis (TNA) documentation.

Your ideas for evidence

Description of evidence	Location of evidence	Opportunities for cross-referencing	Reflection and analysis

K&U links   Suggested reading for knowledge and understanding purposes:

Cole, G.A., *Management: Theory and Practice,* 5th edition, chapters 27 and 44.

Mullins, L.J., *Management and Organisational Behaviour,* 4th edition, chapters 4 and 15.

Needham, D. et al., *Business for Higher Awards,* chapters 10 and 25.

Cross-referencing   Evidence and knowledge from this element can be used in the following mandatory units of NVQ Management Level 3: **A1, C4;** and the following optional unit: **C9.**

Element C1.1 Develop your own skills to improve your performance

Performance Criterion

(e) *You undertake development activities which are consistent with your plans for developing your skills.*

> You can link to PC (d), if appropriate. Detail the development you have undertaken, for example: appraisal, project work, job rotation, shadowing, coaching, mentoring, NVQ or training courses. Explain how undertaking these kinds of activity have helped you develop your skills.

Interpretation

- What kinds of development activity have you undertaken?
- How have they helped you to develop the skills you need?

Candidate illustration

Event route
Both Graham and Emma submitted as evidence the programmes from the training events they had attended. In addition, Graham included a personal action plan, completed during the training event, which outlined the actions he intended to take on his return to the workplace. The evidence and its relevance was clearly explained in their analyses.

Ideas for evidence

- Examples of activities undertaken during training events.
- Programmes of events from development activities.
- Personal reports detailing the development activity.

Your ideas for evidence

Description of evidence	Location of evidence	Opportunities for cross-referencing	Reflection and analysis

K&U links

Suggested reading for knowledge and understanding purposes:

Cole, G.A., *Management: Theory and Practice,* 5th edition, chapters 27 and 44.

Needham, D. et al., *Business for Higher Awards,* chapters 10 and 25.

Cross-referencing

Evidence and knowledge from this element can be used in the following mandatory units of NVQ Management Level 3: **A1, C4**; and the following optional unit: **C9**.

Element C1.1   Develop your own skills to improve your performance

Performance Criterion

(f)   You obtain feedback from relevant people and use it to enhance your performance in the future.

> You should focus on specific instances where you have obtained feedback on your performance. Detail the feedback and explain how you used it to improve. Relevant people should include two of the following throughout this element: team members, peers, higher-level managers, or sponsors and specialists.

Interpretation

- How do you obtain feedback on your performance?
- Who do you obtain it from and why?
- How do you use it to improve your skills and performance?

Candidate illustration

Event route
After cascading the team-building and motivation training to his team, Graham distributed evaluation forms to all those who attended, requesting feedback on content, style of delivery and perceived value of the event. Graham collated responses and used them to gauge the usefulness of the activity, his performance during the cascade training and his team's ability to work cohesively. The evaluation forms were used as evidence and Graham clearly explained their utility in his analysis.

Event route
As part of the time management course that Emma attended (see PC (c)), she was required to keep a personal log detailing her actions and the time spent performing them. At the end of the course the log was submitted, along with a written account, to the course tutor, who provided written feedback pointing out how Emma could manage her time more effectively. Emma continued to log her actions over a few weeks to enable her to improve her time management skills. The original and subsequent logs, which were dated, were submitted as evidence, together with the tutor feedback. Emma clearly explained the circumstances in her analysis.

Ideas for evidence

- Cross-reference to existing evidence used for this unit, if relevant.
- Examples of written feedback that you have recorded.
- Evaluations of performance.
- Completed appraisal documentation.
- Completed supervision documentation.

Your ideas for evidence

Description of evidence	Location of evidence	Opportunities for cross-referencing	Reflection and analysis

K&U links

Suggested reading for knowledge and understanding purposes:

Cole, G.A., *Management: Theory and Practice,* 5th edition, chapters 27 and 44.

Mullins, L.J., *Management and Organisational Behaviour,* 4th edition, chapters 4 and 15.

Needham, D. et al., *Business for Higher Awards,* chapters 10 and 25.

Cross-referencing

Evidence and knowledge from this element can be used in the following mandatory units of NVQ Management Level 3: **A1**, **C4**; and the following optional unit: **C9**.

Element C1.1   Develop your own skills to improve your performance

Performance Criterion

(g) *You update your plans for developing your skills at appropriate intervals.*

> You can link to previous evidence used in this element, if appropriate. Show that you continuously update your personal development plans. Explain how you do this and the information and feedback used to identify new areas for development. Detail the timescales involved and how they are significant. Give examples of updated plans.

Interpretation

■ What information do you use to update your personal development plans?

■ When do you do this?

■ Why are these times appropriate?

Candidate illustration

Event route
Both Graham and Emma were able to cross-reference to the evidence used for PC (a) of this element. The dates of Graham's supervision documents and Emma's personal development portfolio (PDP) were highlighted to show plans being developed over a significant period of time.

Ideas for evidence

■ Cross-reference to existing evidence used for this element, if appropriate.

■ Details of development plans that have been updated over a period of time.

Your ideas for evidence

Description of evidence	Location of evidence	Opportunities for cross-referencing	Reflection and analysis

K&U links

Suggested reading for knowledge and understanding purposes:

Cole, G.A., *Management: Theory and Practice*, 5th edition, chapters 27 and 44.

Mullins, L.J., *Management and Organisational Behaviour*, 4th edition, chapters 4 and 15.

Needham, D. et al., *Business for Higher Awards*, chapters 10 and 25.

Cross-referencing

Evidence and knowledge from this element can be used in the following mandatory units of NVQ Management Level 3: **A1, C4**; and the following optional unit: **C9**.

Element C1.2 Manage your time to meet your objectives

Performance Criterion

(a) *Your objectives are specific, measurable and achievable.*

You will need to explain clearly how you identify and agree your objectives. Detail what your objectives entail and demonstrate that they are realistic.

Interpretation

- What kinds of personal work-related objectives do you set?
- How are they identified and agreed?
- Are they clearly defined?
- How do you ensure that they are realistic?
- How do you qualify them?

Candidate illustration

Event route

Graham focused on his personal administration systems to meet the requirements of this performance criterion. He evidenced his methods of achieving objectives through the use of 'to do' lists, which highlighted the objective and listed the tasks that needed to be completed in order to achieve it. Using this pro-forma, Graham was able to prioritise his work and apply timescales to achievement. A selection of 'to do' lists was included as evidence.

Event route

Emma cross-referenced to the work she used as evidence for Unit A1, Element A1.3, PC (a), where she was working on the night shift project. As part of the project, Emma had to identify specific, time-limited objectives and milestones. These were approved by her manager in supervision. The objectives and the relevant supervision document were included as evidence.

Ideas for evidence

- Examples of written objectives:
  - work priorities and plans;
  - project plans;
  - supervision documentation;
  - personal development plans;
  - team plans.

Your ideas for evidence

Description of evidence	Location of evidence	Opportunities for cross-referencing	Reflection and analysis

K&U links

Suggested reading for knowledge and understanding purposes:

Cole, G.A., *Management: Theory and Practice*, 5th edition, chapter 27.

Mullins, L.J., *Management and Organisational Behaviour*, 4th edition, chapter 13, pp. 460–5.

Needham, D. et al., *Business for Higher Awards*, chapter 11.

Cross-referencing

Evidence and knowledge from this element can be used in any of the mandatory and optional units of NVQ Management Level 3.

Element C1.2 Manage your time to meet your objectives

Performance Criterion

(b) You prioritise your objectives in line with organisational objectives and policies.

You must explain how your objectives are prioritised. Detail the local and broader organisational objectives and any policies that impact on how you prioritise your managerial objectives.

Interpretation

- How do you prioritise your objectives?

- Which organisational objectives and policies have informed the prioritisation of your objectives?

Candidate illustration

Event route

Graham cross-referenced to the evidence he used for PC (a) of this element. In his analysis he detailed the objectives included and explained how they were prioritised. He obtained a witness testimony from his line manager confirming that they complied with and supported the organisation's objectives. Graham also included a copy of the organisation's yearly objectives to show how his objectives supported them.

Event route

Emma continued to cross-reference to Unit A1, Element A1.3, where she was managing the night shift project. She highlighted her remit to investigate the feasibility of beginning a night shift to cope with fluctuations in demand at different times of the year. In her analysis, she explained that her initial project supported the organisational objective of establishing a night shift.

Ideas for evidence

- Cross-reference to existing evidence, if appropriate.

- Details of your objectives.

- Details of organisational objectives and policies.

- Personal statement/witness testimony explaining how the two complement each other.

Your ideas for evidence

Description of evidence	Location of evidence	Opportunities for cross-referencing	Reflection and analysis

K&U links

Suggested reading for knowledge and understanding purposes:

Cole, G.A., *Management: Theory and Practice,* 5th edition, chapter 27.

Mullins, L.J., *Management and Organisational Behaviour,* 4th edition, chapter 13, pp. 460–5.

Needham, D. et al., *Business for Higher Awards,* chapter 11.

Cross-referencing

Evidence and knowledge from this element can be used in any of the mandatory and optional units of NVQ Management Level 3.

Element C1.2 **Manage your time to meet your objectives**

Performance Criterion

(c) *You plan activities which are consistent with your objectives and your personal resources.*

> To meet the requirements of this performance criterion, you will need to explain how you plan your work to meet your objectives. Make sure you detail the resources involved.

Interpretation

■ How do you plan your work?

■ How do you ensure that your work activities will meet your objectives?

■ What are your personal resources?

■ How do you ensure that your work activities will be achievable given the personal resources available?

Candidate illustration

Event route
Graham again cross-referenced to the 'to do' lists used for PCs (a) and (b) of this element. The lists were dated and showed that Graham consistently planned his work to meet objectives. He highlighted several activities and the objectives to which they related, explaining the resources required in his analysis.

Event route
Emma continued to cross-reference to the night shift project referenced for PC (a) of this element. She highlighted her plans for research and the work carried out in the final project report. The tasks were time-limited to allow Emma to allocate time in addition to undertaking her routine job role. This was clearly explained in her analysis.

Ideas for evidence

■ Cross-reference to existing evidence, if appropriate.

■ Work plans.

■ Project outlines.

■ Diary extracts.

Your ideas for evidence

Description of evidence	Location of evidence	Opportunities for cross-referencing	Reflection and analysis

K&U links

Suggested reading for knowledge and understanding purposes:

Cole, G.A., *Management: Theory and Practice,* 5th edition, chapter 27.

Mullins, L.J., *Management and Organisational Behaviour,* 4th edition, chapter 13, pp. 460–5.

Needham, D. et al., *Business for Higher Awards,* chapter 11.

Cross-referencing

Evidence and knowledge from this element can be used in any of the mandatory and optional units of NVQ Management Level 3.

Element C1.2   Manage your time to meet your objectives

Performance Criterion

(d) Your estimates of the time you need for activities are realistic and allow for unforeseen circumstances.

> You will need to explain and evidence how you allocate time to your work activities. For instance, how are timescales calculated? Detail specific instances where you have established timescales for a particular work activity, allowing for unexpected deviations.

Interpretation

- How do you allocate timescales to work activities?
- How do you ensure that these are realistic?

Candidate illustration

Event route
Graham was able to cross-reference to the evidence used for PC (c) of this element. Details of timescales were explained in the analysis of evidence.

Event route
Emma included the Gantt (planning) chart used for her night shift project as evidence. It highlighted timescales and the gaps between specific tasks associated with the project. In her analysis, Emma explained that these gaps allowed for delays in progress.

Ideas for evidence

- Cross-reference to existing evidence, if appropriate.
- Work plans.
- Project outlines.
- Diary extracts.
- Witness testimony from others involved.

Your ideas for evidence

Description of evidence	Location of evidence	Opportunities for cross-referencing	Reflection and analysis

K&U links

Suggested reading for knowledge and understanding purposes:

Cole, G.A., *Management: Theory and Practice,* 5th edition, chapter 27.

Mullins, L.J., *Management and Organisational Behaviour,* 4th edition, chapter 13, pp. 460–5.

Needham, D. et al., *Business for Higher Awards,* chapter 11.

Cross-referencing

Evidence and knowledge from this element can be used in any of the mandatory and optional units of NVQ Management Level 3.

Element C1.2 Manage your time to meet your objectives

Performance Criterion

(e) You take decisions as soon as you have specific information.

> You will have to detail specific instances where you have taken decisions. These can be routine or non-routine decisions. Highlight your decision-making process and explain the information you have used during the process. Detail the timescales involved and their significance.

Interpretation

- When do you make decisions?
- What kinds of information do you use to inform decision taking?
- What are the timescales involved?

Candidate illustration

Event route

Graham detailed a situation where he was required to allocate a resident to a new key worker. Before doing so he collected information regarding the current workloads, experience and availability of existing key workers. He then matched the resident's requirements, based on her care plan, to the most appropriate key worker. Key worker details, together with the resident's care plan, were submitted as evidence. Graham explained this decision-making process in his analysis of evidence.

Event route

Emma cross-referenced to her project report concerning the new night shift, highlighting the recommendations section. She also highlighted the information collected concerning timescales, shift patterns, staff availability and cost implications. In her analysis she linked the two items of evidence together, explaining how the information led her to make the recommendations. Emma's assessor was not convinced that a recommendation constituted a decision. Nevertheless, after additional questioning her assessor decided to deem her competent.

Ideas for evidence

- Cross-reference to existing evidence, if appropriate.
- Items of information.
- Evidence showing decisions that were made, based on the above.
- Reports containing analysis of information, conclusions and recommendations.

Your ideas for evidence

Description of evidence	Location of evidence	Opportunities for cross-referencing	Reflection and analysis

K&U links

Suggested reading for knowledge and understanding purposes:

Cole, G.A., *Management: Theory and Practice,* 5th edition, chapter 27.

Mullins, L.J., *Management and Organisational Behaviour,* 4th edition, chapter 13, pp. 460–5.

Needham, D. et al., *Business for Higher Awards,* chapter 11.

Cross-referencing

Evidence and knowledge from this element can be used in any of the mandatory and optional units of NVQ Management Level 3.

Element C1.2   Manage your time to meet your objectives

<table>
<tr><td>

Performance Criterion

</td><td>

(f)   *You minimise unhelpful interruptions to, and digressions from, planned work.*

You can link to previous performance evidence used in this element, if appropriate. Detail instances where planned work has been interrupted. Explain the nature of the work interruption and the actions you took when dealing with the situation.

</td></tr>
</table>

Interpretation

■   What kinds of interruptions and digressions have occurred?

■   What effect have they had on planned work activities?

■   What actions have you taken to ensure that, despite interruptions, planned work is not delayed?

Candidate illustration

Event route

Graham highlighted an event detailed in one of his 'to do' lists (see PC (a)) concerning a stock-take of all the prescribed medication held at the establishment. The stock-take was delayed due to an influx of new residents and had to be restarted because additional drugs were being prescribed. Graham delayed the stock-take until he was able to identify the days when there would be no change to resident numbers and when each had their full prescription. He thus ensured that the stock-take was accurate. For evidence, Graham included both the obsolete and current stock-take documents. He explained the events and his actions in his analysis and obtained a supporting witness testimony from his line manager.

Event route

Emma continued to focus on her night shift project. During the research phase, Emma's work was delayed because a key member of the management team was absent through illness. She contacted her manager directly at home and requested to meet her out of work hours to avoid delaying the project. Emma included a diary extract showing the meeting and the notes taken. She also obtained a testimony from her line manager confirming her actions.

Ideas for evidence

■   Cross-reference to existing evidence used in the NVQ, if appropriate.

■   Details of delays due to timescales, availability of resources, staff absence.

■   Examples of actions taken.

■   Supporting witness testimony from others involved.

Your ideas for evidence

Description of evidence	Location of evidence	Opportunities for cross-referencing	Reflection and analysis

K&U links Suggested reading for knowledge and understanding purposes:

Cole, G.A., *Management: Theory and Practice,* 5th edition, chapter 27.

Mullins, L.J., *Management and Organisational Behaviour,* 4th edition, chapter 13, pp. 460–5.

Needham, D. et al., *Business for Higher Awards,* chapter 11.

Cross-referencing Evidence and knowledge from this element can be used in any of the mandatory and optional units of NVQ Management Level 3.

| *Element C1.2* | # Manage your time to meet your objectives |

Performance Criterion

(g) *You regularly review progress and reschedule activities to help achieve your planned objectives.*

> You should explain how you review planned work activities against timescales and the achievement of your objectives. Give specific examples where the reviewing process has highlighted the need to change plans. Explain the actions you have taken to ensure that objectives are still achieved.

Interpretation

■ How is progress reviewed?

■ What has been the outcome of the reviewing process?

■ What actions have you taken to ensure that objectives are still achieved?

Candidate illustration

Event route
Both Graham and Emma referred to evidence and analysis submitted for the previous performance criterion (PC (f)).

Ideas for evidence

■ Cross-reference to existing evidence used in the NVQ, if appropriate.

■ Progress review documentation:
  – supervision;
  – appraisal;
  – work plans.

Your ideas for evidence

Description of evidence	Location of evidence	Opportunities for cross-referencing	Reflection and analysis

K&U links   Suggested reading for knowledge and understanding purposes:

Cole, G.A., *Management: Theory and Practice,* 5th edition, chapter 27.

Mullins, L.J., *Management and Organisational Behaviour,* 4th edition, chapter 13, pp. 460–5.

Needham, D. et al., *Business for Higher Awards*, chapter 11.

Cross-referencing   Evidence and knowledge from this element can be used in any of the mandatory and optional units of NVQ Management Level 3.

CHAPTER 7

Unit C4 Create effective working relationships

Element C4.3   Minimise conflict in your team

Element C4.1   Gain the support and trust of colleagues and team members

Performance Criterion

(a) *You consult with colleagues and team members about proposed activities at appropriate times and in a manner which encourages open, frank discussion.*

> You will need to detail specific instances where you have discussed work activities with others. Explain your approach, given your knowledge and experience of working with those people. Colleagues should include at least one of the following throughout this element: peers, people working at a higher level than you (superiors), and those working at a lower level than you (subordinates). Team members should include at least one of the following throughout this element: people for whom you have line management responsibility and people for whom you have functional responsibility (i.e. they contribute to the work of your team/section/group, although you may not have managerial responsibility for them).

Interpretation

- When do you consult with others about work activities?
- Why is this an appropriate time?
- How do you consult?
- How do you encourage open and frank discussion?

Candidate illustration

Event route
Graham detailed two examples of the monthly team meetings he chaired. He included agendas and minutes of the meetings as evidence. Graham highlighted instances throughout the meeting, recorded in the minutes, where he had discussed practice issues, new procedures and events in the unit. Some of these new procedures were not received very favourably by the team and the minutes clearly showed a high degree of open, frank discussion! Graham deleted the names of the other team members so as not to jeopardise their trust or support.

Event route
Emma focused on her biannual team review day, a one-day event held away from the workplace which allowed the team to discuss predetermined issues, objectives and plans. Emma led the day and consulted staff and colleagues before each event to establish topic focus areas. As evidence, she included a memo sent to staff and colleagues requesting their input on the issues they felt should be raised, together with the minutes of a team meeting where the event was discussed. Emma explained the team review days and her actions in her analysis, highlighting the period of notice given to staff before the review days to allow them to prepare. Emma also obtained a witness testimony from one of the participants, which confirmed her consultative approach.

Ideas for evidence

■ Agendas of meetings.

■ Memos consulting staff or requesting their input.

■ Details of timescales and their significance.

Your ideas for evidence

Description of evidence	Location of evidence	Opportunities for cross-referencing	Reflection and analysis

K&U links

Suggested reading for knowledge and understanding purposes:

Cole, G.A., *Management: Theory and Practice,* 5th edition, chapters 6, 7, 8 and 27.

Mullins, L.J., *Management and Organisational Behaviour,* 4th edition, chapters 5, 6, 7 and 8.

Needham, D. et al., *Business for Higher Awards,* chapters 10 and 14.

Cross-referencing

Evidence and knowledge from this element can be used in the following mandatory units of NVQ Management Level 3: **A1, B1, C1**; and the following optional units: **C9, C12, C15**.

<table>
<tr><td>

Element **C4.1**
</td><td>

Gain the support and trust of colleagues and team members
</td></tr>
</table>

Performance Criterion

(b) *You keep colleagues and team members informed about organisational plans and objectives.*

> You will need to detail specific instances where you have informed or updated others regarding plans and activities. Remember to explain why this was necessary and detail the circumstances where this took place.

Interpretation

■ How do you keep others updated regarding organisational plans, objectives, strategies, tactics or directives?

■ When has this occurred?

Candidate illustration

Event route
Graham cross-referenced to the evidence used for PC (a) of this element. He highlighted examples of information that he had presented and explained to his team regarding organisation-wide plans and activities.

Event route
Emma took a photograph of the staff notice board, where she displayed organisation-wide memos for staff to read. Staff were also required to sign to confirm that they had read memos and other items of information. The photo was included as evidence, together with an example of a memo and the list that staff signed. In addition, Emma invited her NVQ assessor to visit her workplace to observe the memos and notice board and to talk to staff in order to confirm her actions.

Ideas for evidence

■ Cross-reference to existing evidence, if appropriate.

■ Highlighted minutes of meetings where organisational issues have been discussed with your team.

■ Memos that have been circulated or displayed.

■ Supportive witness testimony from those involved.

■ Records of observational assessment in the workplace.

Your ideas for evidence

Description of evidence	Location of evidence	Opportunities for cross-referencing	Reflection and analysis

K&U links   Suggested reading for knowledge and understanding purposes:

Cole, G.A., *Management: Theory and Practice*, 5th edition, chapters 6, 7, 8 and 27.

Mullins, L.J., *Management and Organisational Behaviour*, 4th edition, chapters 5, 6, 7 and 8.

Needham, D. et al., *Business for Higher Awards*, chapters 10, 11 and 14.

Cross-referencing   Evidence and knowledge from this element can be used in the following mandatory units of NVQ Management Level 3: **A1, B1, C1**; and the following optional units: **C9, C12, C15**.

Gain the support and trust of colleagues and team members

Performance Criterion

(c) *You honour the commitments you make to colleagues and team members.*

> To meet the requirements of this performance criterion, you will need to explain specific circumstances where you have made a commitment to an activity or agreement with others. In addition, you should detail how you ensured that the commitment was met.

Interpretation

◼ In what circumstances have you made commitments to others?

◼ How have you ensured that these were met?

◼ Why is it important to honour commitments to colleagues and team members?

Candidate illustration

Event route
Graham detailed an instance where he had offered to undertake some research in the unit, on behalf of another manager. The work involved compiling a comparative study to identify whether their service was standardised across units. To gather information, Graham used a questionnaire designed for residents. When he had completed the work, Graham received written thanks from the manager of the other unit. An example of a completed questionnaire, together with the letter of thanks, was submitted as evidence. Graham clearly explained his actions in his analysis of the evidence.

Event route
Emma submitted an example of a supervision document for two members of staff who had requested that they swap jobs for six months to gain new skills. The document showed that Emma had agreed in principle but needed authorisation from the production manager. Written consent from the production manager was received and submitted as evidence, together with the supervision document.

Ideas for evidence

◼ Details of undertakings:
  – supervision documents;
  – response to requests;
  – emails;
  – letters;
  – memos.

◼ Confirmation that undertakings were honoured (as above).

◼ Witness testimony from those involved.

Your ideas for evidence

Description of evidence	Location of evidence	Opportunities for cross-referencing	Reflection and analysis

K&U links

Suggested reading for knowledge and understanding purposes:

Cole, G.A., *Management: Theory and Practice*, 5th edition, chapters 6, 7, 8 and 27.

Mullins, L.J., *Management and Organisational Behaviour*, 4th edition, chapters 5, 6, 7 and 8.

Needham, D. et al., *Business for Higher Awards*, chapter 10.

Cross-referencing

Evidence and knowledge from this element can be used in the following mandatory units of NVQ Management Level 3: **A1**, **B1**, **C1**; and the following optional units: **C9**, **C12**, **C15**.

Element C4.1	# Gain the support and trust of colleagues and team members

Performance Criterion

(d) *You treat colleagues and team members in a manner which shows your respect for individuals and the need for confidentiality.*

> You can link to previous evidence used in this element, if appropriate. Explain how you conduct yourself when dealing with others. Detail an instance where you have demonstrated your awareness of the need for confidentiality in dealing with others.

Interpretation

- How do you conduct yourself when dealing with colleagues?
- How do you show respect for individuals in the workplace?
- In what circumstances is confidentiality important in gaining the support and trust of others?

Candidate illustration

Event route
Graham focused on the supervision process and submitted examples of completed supervision records detailing discussions with members of his team. He explained in his analysis that all discussions held during supervision were confidential and records were stored securely. He also submitted a witness testimony from a member of his team confirming the confidentiality of supervision and explaining that supervision occurred at planned times agreed between supervisor and supervisee, in a confidential and relaxed environment.

Event route
Emma focused on a specific incident where she had to consult with a colleague about the performance of a member of staff. She submitted a personal report detailing her actions in setting up the meeting and a diary extract indicating the date, time and place. The colleague also provided a witness testimony confirming that Emma conducted herself in a professional manner when discussing a sensitive issue.

Ideas for evidence

- Link to evidence used in this element, if appropriate.
- Examples of supervision documentation.
- Examples of appraisal documentation.
- Personal reports detailing your actions.
- Supporting witness testimony from others involved.

Your ideas for evidence

Description of evidence	Location of evidence	Opportunities for cross-referencing	Reflection and analysis

K&U links

Suggested reading for knowledge and understanding purposes:

Cole, G.A., *Management: Theory and Practice,* 5th edition, chapters 6, 7, 8 and 27.

Mullins, L.J., *Management and Organisational Behaviour,* 4th edition, chapters 5, 6, 7 and 8.

Needham, D. et al., *Business for Higher Awards,* chapters 10 and 14.

Cross-referencing

Evidence and knowledge from this element can be used in the following mandatory units of NVQ Management Level 3: **A1**, **B1**, **C1**; and the following optional units: **C9, C12, C15.**

Element C4.1   Gain the support and trust of colleagues and team members

Performance Criterion

(e) *You give colleagues and team members sufficient support for them to achieve their work objectives.*

> You can link to previous evidence used in this element, if appropriate. Focus on instances where you have supported others. Explain the objectives they were working towards and how your support assisted them.

Interpretation

■ In what circumstances have you given support to others?

■ What form did this support take?

■ How did your support assist others to achieve their work objectives?

Candidate illustration

Event route
Graham cross-referenced to the supervision documentation used in PC (d) of this element. He highlighted specific sections and action point areas showing his responsibilities in supporting team members in achieving their work objectives. The nature of the support was clearly explained in his analysis.

Event route
Emma continued to focus on the team review day evidence (see PC (a)). She submitted the programme and the notes she made following presentations by each member of her team on their development objectives for the coming six months. The notes contained lists of resources that each member requested. Emma explained that she had agreed to the provision of some of the resources and submitted an email circulated to staff following the review day identifying the specific resources that would be available.

Ideas for evidence

■ Link to previous evidence used in this element, if appropriate.

■ Examples of completed supervision documentation.

■ Examples of support given:
   – minutes of meetings;
   – memos;
   – emails;
   – personal notes.

Your ideas for evidence

Description of evidence	Location of evidence	Opportunities for cross-referencing	Reflection and analysis

K&U links

Suggested reading for knowledge and understanding purposes:

Cole, G.A., *Management: Theory and Practice,* 5th edition, chapters 6, 7, 8 and 27.

Mullins, L.J., *Management and Organisational Behaviour,* 4th edition, chapters 5, 6, 7 and 8.

Needham, D. et al., *Business for Higher Awards,* chapters 10, 11 and 14.

Cross-referencing

Evidence and knowledge from this element can be used in the following mandatory units of NVQ Management Level 3: **A1, B1, C1**; and the following optional units: **C9, C12, C15**.

Element C4.1	# Gain the support and trust of colleagues and team members

Performance Criterion

(f) *You discuss your evaluation of their work and behaviour directly with colleagues and team members concerned.*

> You should explain instances where you have given your professional opinion to others regarding their performance and actions. Detail the area of discussion and how it occurred. The discussion can be formal or informal.

Interpretation

■ When have you discussed work and performance with colleagues and team members?

■ Was this a routine or non-routine event?

■ How did you approach the discussion to ensure that support and trust was gained?

Candidate illustration

Event route
Graham again cross-referenced to the completed monthly supervision documents submitted in support of PC (d) of this element. He highlighted the sections of the documents that reviewed previous targets and the achievement of objectives where notes of discussions with team members were made.

Event route
Emma detailed the quarterly appraisal system used in her organisation. She submitted examples of appraisal feedback documents she had completed and copied to the staff concerned. In her analysis, she explained the nature and circumstances behind the feedback to those concerned.

Ideas for evidence

■ Link to evidence used in this element, if appropriate.

■ Completed supervision documents.

■ Completed appraisal documents.

■ Supportive witness testimony from the team members concerned.

■ Personal report detailing your actions.

Your ideas for evidence

Description of evidence	Location of evidence	Opportunities for cross-referencing	Reflection and analysis

K&U links

Suggested reading for knowledge and understanding purposes:

Cole, G.A., *Management: Theory and Practice,* 5th edition, chapters 6, 7, 8 and 27.

Mullins, L.J., *Management and Organisational Behaviour,* 4th edition, chapters 5, 6, 7 and 8.

Needham, D. et al., *Business for Higher Awards,* chapters 10 and 14.

Cross-referencing

Evidence and knowledge from this element can be used in the following mandatory units of NVQ Management Level 3: **A1**, **B1**, **C1**; and the following optional units: **C9**, **C12**, **C15**.

Element C4.2   Gain the trust and support of your manager

Performance Criterion

(a) *You give your manager timely and accurate reports on activities, progress, results and achievements.*

> You should focus on specific formal or informal instances where you have discussed or presented written reports on your performance with your manager. Explain the significance of the timescales involved. Your manager should be the person to whom you report or the organisation or authority to which you report.

Interpretation

■ When do you provide this kind of information for your manager?

■ Are written reports provided?

■ How do you ensure they are timely and accurate?

Candidate illustration

Event route
Graham focused on the organisation-wide supervision process to meet the requirements of most of this element. He submitted two examples of documents detailing supervision sessions he had had with his manager, highlighting where reports had been given on progress and achievements. Graham explained the process in his analysis of evidence.

Event route
Emma submitted an example of a written progress report that she had presented to her manager. The report concerned estimated production times for a new kind of product that the company was developing. Emma annotated the sections that detailed activities, the development process and anticipated outputs.

Ideas for evidence

■ Supervision documents.

■ Progress reports.

■ Personal reports detailing the actions you have taken.

■ Witness testimony from your manager confirming your actions.

Your ideas for evidence

Description of evidence	Location of evidence	Opportunities for cross-referencing	Reflection and analysis

K&U links

Suggested reading for knowledge and understanding purposes:

Cole, G.A., *Management: Theory and Practice,* 5th edition, chapters 6, 7, 26 and 27.

Mullins, L.J., *Management and Organisational Behaviour,* 4th edition, chapters 4, 5, 8, 10 and 13.

Needham, D. et al., *Business for Higher Awards,* chapters 9, 10, 11 and 14.

Cross-referencing

Evidence and knowledge from this element can be used in the following mandatory units of NVQ Management Level 3: **A1**, **B1**, **C1**; and the following optional units: **C9**, **C12**, **C15**.

Element C4.2 Gain the trust and support of your manager

Performance Criterion

(b) You give your manager clear, accurate and timely information about emerging threats and opportunities.

> You must focus on specific instances where you have provided information of this nature to your manager. Explain the nature of the threats and opportunities, and their implications. Detail the timescales involved.

Interpretation

▌ How have you provided information regarding threats and opportunities?

▌ What were the implications?

▌ Why was your timing appropriate?

Candidate illustration

Event route
Graham continued to focus on the supervision process (see PC (a)). He cross-referenced to the two supervision documents, highlighting them to show opportunities regarding alternative suppliers, and threats because of high levels of staff absence through sickness.

Event route
Emma also cross-referenced to the progress report submitted for PC (a) of this element. She highlighted sections of the report that detailed opportunities for increasing outputs and threats regarding the cost implications of production.

Ideas for evidence

▌ Supervision documentation.

▌ Progress reports.

▌ Notes of discussions with your manager.

▌ Personal reports detailing the actions you have taken.

▌ Witness testimony from your manager confirming your actions.

Your ideas for evidence

Description of evidence	Location of evidence	Opportunities for cross-referencing	Reflection and analysis

K&U links

Suggested reading for knowledge and understanding purposes:

Cole, G.A., *Management: Theory and Practice,* 5th edition, chapters 6, 7, 26 and 27.

Mullins, L.J., *Management and Organisational Behaviour,* 4th edition, chapters 4, 5, 8, 10 and 13.

Needham, D. et al., *Business for Higher Awards,* chapters 9, 10, 11 and 14.

Cross-referencing

Evidence and knowledge from this element can be used in the following mandatory units of NVQ Management Level 3: **A1**, **B1**, **C1**; and the following optional units: **C9**, **C12**, **C15**.

| Element C4.2 | # Gain the trust and support of your manager |

Performance Criterion

(c) You consult your manager about organisational policies and ways of working at appropriate times.

> You will need to focus on specific instances where you have consulted your manager about policy or best practice issues. Detail the circumstances and the issues discussed. Explain any timescales involved.

Interpretation

- When have you consulted your manager regarding policy and practice issues?
- Why did you do this?
- When did this occur?

Candidate illustration

Event route

Graham met with his manager and the other assistant managers to discuss a new policy and procedure regarding the handover period between shifts. The meeting was minuted and the minutes were submitted as evidence, together with the notes Graham took during the meeting.

Event route

After reading some new documentation issued by the Health and Safety Executive, Emma submitted a memo she had sent to her manager requesting information on any changes to health and safety procedures that applied to her production area. She also requested information on safety risk assessment documentation. Her manager discussed the issues with her in supervision and the notes taken were submitted as evidence.

Ideas for evidence

- Link to evidence used in this element, if appropriate.
- Notes and minutes of meetings with your manager.
- Memos sent and received.
- Supervision documents.

Your ideas for evidence

Description of evidence	Location of evidence	Opportunities for cross-referencing	Reflection and analysis

K&U links

Suggested reading for knowledge and understanding purposes:

Cole, G.A., *Management: Theory and Practice,* 5th edition, chapters 6, 7, 26 and 27.

Mullins, L.J., *Management and Organisational Behaviour,* 4th edition, chapters 4, 5, 8, 10 and 13.

Needham, D. et al., *Business for Higher Awards,* chapters 10, 11 and 14.

Cross-referencing

Evidence and knowledge from this element can be used in the following mandatory units of NVQ Management Level 3: **A1**, **B1**, **C1**; and the following optional units: **C9**, **C12**, **C15**.

Element C4.2	# Gain the trust and support of your manager

Performance Criterion

(d) Your proposals for action are clear and realistic.

You should evidence and explain specific proposals for action that you have written or explained to your manager. Detail how you ensured that your proposals were understandable and realistic. Throughout the element, proposals may be either spoken or written.

Interpretation

■ How do you compile proposals?

■ Have they been spoken or written?

■ What factors do you consider when ensuring that your proposals are understandable and realistic?

Candidate illustration

Event route
Graham highlighted the supervision documents used in PCs (a) and (b) of this element to show his proposal and the action to be taken to achieve his short-term objectives. These were clearly agreed by his manager.

Event route
Emma cross-referenced to the progress report used for PCs (a) and (b) of this element. The report made recommendations for progress and sought agreement from her line manager. Emma detailed the significance of the timescales involved in her analysis.

Ideas for evidence

■ Link to previous evidence used in this element, if appropriate.

■ Notes and minutes of meetings held with your manager.

■ Supervision documentation.

■ Reports making proposals for action.

Your ideas for evidence

Description of evidence	Location of evidence	Opportunities for cross-referencing	Reflection and analysis

K&U links

Suggested reading for knowledge and understanding purposes:

Cole, G.A., *Management: Theory and Practice,* 5th edition, chapters 6, 7, 26 and 27.

Mullins, L.J., *Management and Organisational Behaviour,* 4th edition, chapters 4, 5, 8, 10 and 13.

Needham, D. et al., *Business for Higher Awards,* chapters 11 and 14.

Cross-referencing

Evidence and knowledge from this element can be used in the following mandatory units of NVQ Management Level 3: **A1**, **B1**, **C1**; and the following optional units: **C9**, **C12**, **C15**.

Element C4.2 Gain the trust and support of your manager

Performance Criterion

(e) *You present your proposals for action to your manager at appropriate times.*

> You could link to the evidence used for the previous performance criterion, if appropriate. You must make sure that you explain how your proposals are presented and the significance of the timescales involved.

Interpretation

▪ How are your proposals presented?

▪ What is the significance of the timescales involved?

Candidate illustration

Event route
Both Graham and Emma cross-referenced to the evidence used in PC (a) of this element. Graham also included a personal statement explaining the supervision process and the planning of supervision over the year. Emma obtained a witness testimony from her line manager confirming that her report was presented within agreed timescales.

Ideas for evidence

▪ Link to previous evidence used in this element, if appropriate.

▪ Details of agreed timescales.

▪ Diary extracts.

▪ Personal statement detailing the timescales involved.

▪ Witness testimony from your line manager confirming your actions.

Your ideas for evidence

Description of evidence	Location of evidence	Opportunities for cross-referencing	Reflection and analysis

K&U links

Suggested reading for knowledge and understanding purposes:

Cole, G.A., *Management: Theory and Practice,* 5th edition, chapters 6, 7, 26 and 27.

Mullins, L.J., *Management and Organisational Behaviour,* 4th edition, chapters 4, 5, 8, 10 and 13.

Needham, D. et al., *Business for Higher Awards,* chapters 11 and 14.

Cross-referencing

Evidence and knowledge from this element can be used in the following mandatory units of NVQ Management Level 3: **A1**, **B1**, **C1**; and the following optional units: **C9**, **C12**, **C15**.

Element C4.2 Gain the trust and support of your manager

Performance Criterion

(f) Where you have disagreements with your manager, you make constructive efforts to resolve the disagreements.

You should focus upon a specific instance where you and your manager have disagreed over work-based issues. Explain the actions that you took to resolve the disagreement without compromising your relationship and to maintain trust and support.

Interpretation

- In what circumstances have you and your manager disagreed over work-based issues?
- How was the disagreement resolved?
- What action was taken?
- How did you act to ensure that your relationship was not compromised?

Candidate illustration

Event route
Graham detailed an incident where he had disagreed with his manager over a complaint made by a resident about one of Graham's team. Graham's manager wanted to ignore the complaint but Graham felt that this was not the best course of action. Graham expressed his concerns in a memo to his manager and arranged a meeting to discuss the conduct of the member of staff. The matter was resolved and disciplinary action avoided by Graham, who offered to provide additional training and support to the member of staff. This was noted by Graham's manager and reviewed at the next supervision session. The memo, notes of the meeting and the supervision review were submitted as evidence. Graham also included a witness testimony from his manager confirming that he acted in a professional manner throughout the incident.

Event route
Emma detailed an incident where her manager had rejected her proposals for planned production outputs on the basis that they were not achievable. Emma met with her manager to discuss the situation and requested a two-week trial period, using her production figures as targets, to test their achievability. Emma's manager agreed, subject to Emma providing daily rather than weekly production figures to enable positive and negative variances from planned outputs to be quickly identified. Emma explained in her analysis that in taking this approach, a compromise was agreed. The notes from the meeting were submitted as evidence, together with examples of the daily production output reports that Emma sent to her manager.

Ideas for evidence

▊ Simulation, such as a 'What I would do if...' report or role play, is acceptable as evidence for this performance criterion.

▊ Details of conflicts and how they are resolved.

▊ Memos sent to, and received from, your manager.

▊ Supervision records.

▊ Outcomes of the resolution:
  – reports;
  – activities;
  – actions taken;
  – agreements.

Your ideas for evidence

Description of evidence	Location of evidence	Opportunities for cross-referencing	Reflection and analysis

K&U links

Suggested reading for knowledge and understanding purposes:

Cole, G.A., *Management: Theory and Practice,* 5th edition, chapters 6, 7, 26 and 27.

Mullins, L.J., *Management and Organisational Behaviour,* 4th edition, chapters 4, 5, 8, 10 and 13.

Needham, D. et al., *Business for Higher Awards,* chapters 10, 11 and 14.

Cross-referencing

Evidence and knowledge from this element can be used in the following mandatory units of NVQ Management Level 3: **A1**, **B1**, **C1**; and the following optional units: **C9**, **C12**, **C15**.

Element C4.3   Minimise conflict in your team

Performance Criterion

(a) *You inform team members of the standards of work and behaviour you expect, in a manner and at a level and pace appropriate to the individuals concerned.*

> You will need to explain how you ensure that the members of your team know what is expected of them. Highlight how this information is provided and how you check team members' understanding of what is required.

Interpretation

◾ How do you inform individual team members of what is expected of them?

◾ How do you ensure that they understand the expectations?

◾ Do you use your knowledge of the individuals concerned to inform your approach?

Candidate illustration

Event route
Graham focused on induction procedures for new employees, for which he was responsible. Following the induction process, an induction checklist was signed by Graham and by the new employee to confirm receipt. Graham explained the process in his analysis. As evidence, he submitted an example of a completed and signed induction checklist and conditions of service, job role, policies and procedures, and health and safety guidelines. Graham also included a personal statement detailing his approach to induction and new employees. In it he explained that he did not assume prior knowledge, avoided the use of jargon and took a supportive approach to induction.

Event route
Emma focused on the supervision process and submitted several supervision documents for three members of her team. She obtained their permission before using the documents and deleted their names in order to maintain confidentiality. She highlighted specific sections from the documents where standards of work and behaviour were discussed. Issues included time keeping, health and safety, production-line working and taking breaks. Emma explained the circumstances behind each discussion and the approach that she adopted in a personal statement.

Ideas for evidence

◾ Evidence drawn from the induction process.

◾ Supervision documentation.

◾ Appraisal documentation.

◾ Personal reports detailing your actions and approach.

◾ Witness testimony from team members involved.

Your ideas for evidence

Description of evidence	Location of evidence	Opportunities for cross-referencing	Reflection and analysis

K&U links

Suggested reading for knowledge and understanding purposes:

Cole, G.A., *Management: Theory and Practice,* 5th edition, chapter 26.

Mullins, L.J., *Management and Organisational Behaviour,* 4th edition, chapters 4, 5, 6 and 7, chapter 20, pp. 722–8.

Needham, D. et al., *Business for Higher Awards,* chapters 10 and 14.

Cross-referencing

Evidence and knowledge from this element can be used in the following mandatory units of NVQ Management Level 3: **A1**, **B1**; and the following optional units: **C9**, **C12**, **C15**.

Element C4.3   Minimise conflict in your team

Performance Criterion

(b) You provide appropriate opportunities for team members to discuss problems which directly or indirectly affect their work.

> You should explain how you provide formal and informal opportunities for discussing problems with team members. Detail specific examples. Across the element, team members should be people for whom you have line management responsibility or people for whom you have functional responsibility.

Interpretation

▪ How are opportunities for discussing problems provided?

▪ Are these formal or informal?

▪ What actions do you take to ensure that these kinds of opportunities are provided?

Candidate illustration

Event route
Both Graham and Emma focused on the supervision procedures used in their organisations. Graham cross-referenced to Element C4.1, PC (d), where he had held discussions with individuals regarding problems and their resolution. He highlighted the relevant parts of the supervision documents and explained the circumstances in his analysis.

Event route
Emma cross-referenced to the evidence used for PC (a) of this element, highlighting the problem areas and issues raised by team members during supervision. Her actions were clearly explained in her analysis of evidence.

Ideas for evidence

▪ Link to previous evidence used in this element or cross-reference to other evidence used in the NVQ, if appropriate.

▪ Details of instances where you have formally or informally discussed problem areas with staff:
   – completed supervision documentation;
     notes of informal discussions;
   – notes from counselling sessions with staff (obtain permission and delete names);
   – minutes of team meetings that explore common problems.

Your ideas for evidence

Description of evidence	Location of evidence	Opportunities for cross-referencing	Reflection and analysis

K&U links   Suggested reading for knowledge and understanding purposes:

Cole, G.A., *Management: Theory and Practice,* 5th edition, chapter 26.

Mullins, L.J., *Management and Organisational Behaviour,* 4th edition, chapters 4, 5, 6 and 7, chapter 20, pp. 722–8.

Needham, D. et al., *Business for Higher Awards,* chapters 10 and 14.

Cross-referencing   Evidence and knowledge from this element can be used in the following mandatory units of NVQ Management Level 3: **A1**, **B1**; and the following optional units: **C9**, **C12**, **C15**.

Element C4.3   Minimise conflict in your team

Performance Criterion

(c) You take action promptly to deal with conflict between team members.

> You will need to focus on a specific instance where conflict has arisen between members of your team. Make sure you clearly explain the action that you have taken in dealing with it.

Interpretation

- In what circumstances has conflict arisen between members of your team?
- What action have you taken to deal with or resolve the conflict?

Candidate illustration

Event route
Graham focused on a specific instance where two team members agreed to swap shifts and one was unable to cover for the other owing to personal problems. Since their conduct was affecting the working environment, Graham met with both staff members to define the problem. He encouraged them to identify and agree a solution and to formulate an action plan for putting it into practice. He included the action plan, signed by all of those involved, as evidence, together with a witness testimony from the staff members confirming his actions.

Event route
Emma detailed a conflict over the late arrival of a particular member of staff and its effect on the production line and other team members. Emma discussed the problem with the member of staff, and solutions to the personal issues involved were identified. Emma's line manager had also been informed of the conflict, so Emma sent him a memo explaining the situation and the actions taken. This was submitted as evidence.

Ideas for evidence

- Simulation, such as a 'What I would do if...' report or role play, is acceptable as evidence for this performance criterion.
- Personal report detailing specific conflict situations that you have managed.
- Action plans relating to conflict resolution.
- Memos regarding conflicts sent to others involved.
- Witness testimony from the team members involved.

Your ideas for evidence

Description of evidence	Location of evidence	Opportunities for cross-referencing	Reflection and analysis

K&U links

Suggested reading for knowledge and understanding purposes:

Cole, G.A., *Management: Theory and Practice,* 5th edition, chapter 26.

Mullins, L.J., *Management and Organisational Behaviour,* 4th edition, chapters 4, 5, 6 and 7, chapter 20, pp. 722–8.

Needham, D. et al., *Business for Higher Awards,* chapters 10 and 14.

Cross-referencing

Evidence and knowledge from this element can be used in the following mandatory units of NVQ Management Level 3: **A1, B1**; and the following optional units: **C9, C12, C15**.

Element C4.3 # Minimise conflict in your team

Performance Criterion

(d) *You inform relevant people about conflicts outside your area of responsibility.*

> You must explain specific instances where you have noticed conflicts between individuals who are not part of your team or responsibility. Detail the nature of the occurrence and explain the action that you took in informing the relevant people.

Interpretation

▪ In what circumstances have you noticed conflict between people who are not part of your team or responsibility?

▪ Who did you inform of the conflict?

▪ Why were they the relevant people to inform?

Candidate illustration

Event route
Graham detailed an instance where a shift handover had resulted in a conflict between two staff members over care provided to a resident. Graham had responsibility for one member of staff concerned and discussed the conflict with his colleague, another assistant manager who was responsible for the other individual involved. The four met to resolve the conflict, putting the interests of the resident first. Graham submitted a personal report detailing the conflict and his actions. He also obtained a witness testimony from his colleague confirming the approach to resolving the conflict.

Event route
During a night shift, Emma was shocked to witness a physical conflict between two members of security staff. She immediately telephoned the on-duty security manager at the gatehouse, who dealt with the incident. Emma obtained a witness testimony from him, confirming her prompt and appropriate action.

Ideas for evidence

▪ Simulation, such as a 'What I would do if…' report or role play, is acceptable as evidence for this performance criterion.

▪ Link to existing evidence used in this element, if appropriate.

▪ Details of discussion of conflicts with others involved.

▪ Memos and correspondence sent or received.

▪ Personal report detailing your actions.

▪ Witness testimony from relevant people confirming your actions.

Your ideas for evidence

Description of evidence	Location of evidence	Opportunities for cross-referencing	Reflection and analysis

K&U links   Suggested reading for knowledge and understanding purposes:

Cole, G.A., *Management: Theory and Practice*, 5th edition, chapter 26.

Mullins, L.J., *Management and Organisational Behaviour*, 4th edition, chapters 4, 5, 6 and 7, chapter 20, pp. 722–8.

Needham, D. et al., *Business for Higher Awards*, chapters 10 and 14.

Cross-referencing   Evidence and knowledge from this element can be used in the following mandatory units of NVQ Management Level 3: **A1**, **B1**; and the following optional units: **C9**, **C12**, **C15**.

Element C4.3   Minimise conflict in your team

Performance Criterion

(e) *The way you resolve conflict minimises disruption to work and discord between team members.*

> You could link to evidence used in other performance criteria in this element, if appropriate. Detail specific instances where you have been involved in resolving a conflict. Explain the actions you took to ensure that work was not disrupted and that the team continued to work well together.

Interpretation

◼ Have you resolved conflicts?

◼ What skills have you used to ensure that the team continued to function effectively?

◼ How did you ensure that work patterns and achievement were not disrupted?

Candidate illustration

Event route
Graham and Emma cross-referenced to the evidence used for PC (c) of this element, as the evidence already demonstrated how they resolved the conflicts. In their analysis, they explained their approach to minimising disruption to other team members and work plans.

Ideas for evidence

◼ Simulation, such as a 'What I would do if...' report or role play, is acceptable as evidence for this performance criterion.

◼ Cross-reference or link to existing evidence used in this element, if appropriate.

◼ Personal report detailing specific conflict situations that you have managed.

◼ Notes of discussions held with those involved.

◼ Action plans relating to conflict resolution.

◼ Memos regarding conflicts.

◼ Witness testimony from others involved.

Your ideas for evidence

Description of evidence	Location of evidence	Opportunities for cross-referencing	Reflection and analysis

K&U links

Suggested reading for knowledge and understanding purposes:

Cole, G.A., *Management: Theory and Practice,* 5th edition, chapter 26.

Mullins, L.J., *Management and Organisational Behaviour,* 4th edition, chapters 4, 5, 6 and 7, chapter 20, pp. 722–8.

Needham, D. et al., *Business for Higher Awards,* chapters 10 and 14.

Cross-referencing

Evidence and knowledge from this element can be used in the following mandatory units of NVQ Management Level 3: **A1, B1**; and the following optional units: **C9, C12, C15**.

Element C4.3   Minimise conflict in your team

Performance Criterion

(f)   Records of conflicts and their outcomes are accurate and comply with requirements for confidentiality and other organisational policies.

> To meet the requirements of this performance criterion you will need to make reference to specific records used for recording conflicts and actions taken. Explain how they are maintained – focus on any organisational policies and procedures that inform their storage, maintenance and use.

Interpretation

■ What kinds of records that monitor conflict are kept?

■ What are they used for?

■ What policies and procedures impact on these kinds of records, their storage and use?

Candidate illustration

Event route
Graham cross-referenced to Element C4.1, PC (d), where he had included specific documents detailing the problems discussed with team members. In his analysis he detailed the supervision process, confidentiality issues and the storage of supervision documents.

Event route
Emma explained in her analysis that conflict records were not kept as part of organisational procedures. She explained that conflicts had been dealt with in supervision with team members, submitting examples of supervision documents as evidence. Emma also created a sample document that could be used to record conflicts in future, if necessary. This was also submitted as evidence and explained.

Ideas for evidence

■ Simulation, such as a created set of documents with explanations, is acceptable as evidence for this performance criterion.

■ Cross-reference or link to existing evidence used in this unit, if appropriate.

■ Supervision documentation.

■ Action plans relating to conflict resolution and solutions.

Your ideas for evidence

Description of evidence	Location of evidence	Opportunities for cross-referencing	Reflection and analysis

K&U links   Suggested reading for knowledge and understanding purposes:

Cole, G.A., *Management: Theory and Practice*, 5th edition, chapter 26.

Mullins, L.J., *Management and Organisational Behaviour*, 4th edition, chapters 4, 5, 6 and 7, chapter 20, pp. 722–8.

Needham, D. et al., *Business for Higher Awards*, chapters 10, 14, 24 and 25.

Cross-referencing   Evidence and knowledge from this element can be used in the following mandatory units of NVQ Management Level 3: **A1, B1**; and the following optional units: **C9, C12, C15**.

CHAPTER 8

Unit D1 Manage information for action

Element D1.3 Hold meetings

Element D1.1 Gather required information

Performance Criterion

(a) The information you gather is accurate, sufficient and relevant to the purpose for which it is needed.

> You will need to detail a specific instance where you have gathered information for a specific purpose. Explain why the information was needed and the relevance of what you gathered. Make sure you put the evidence into context. Information should be quantitative (number-based) and qualitative (word-based) throughout this element.

Interpretation

- When have you needed to gather information?
- Why was it needed?
- How did you ensure relevance and sufficiency?

Candidate illustration

Event route
Throughout this element, Graham detailed a routine function. He focused on his responsibility for monitoring, recording and forwarding bed occupancy information to the central office. For this PC, Graham detailed examples of bed occupancy report sheets that he had to complete on a weekly basis. In his analysis Graham explained why this information was needed and submitted examples of the sheets as evidence. His methods of collecting the information were also clearly explained in a personal statement.

Event route
Throughout this element, Emma focused on her involvement and responsibilities in the ISO 9000 quality assurance working party. She explained that the group was formed to research, develop and implement organisational systems that complied with the standard so that the company could be accredited with ISO 9000. Her initial remit was to collect information on the standard and on its implementation specific to the part of the production process for which she was responsible. She obtained the standard and relevant details about implementation through her local Business Link office. Examples of the information were submitted as evidence, with dates of publication highlighted to show currency. Emma clearly explained her actions in her analysis of the evidence.

Ideas for evidence

- Examples of information collected, highlighting content, dates obtained and sources.
- Personal statement explaining your methods of information collection.
- Details of your routine responsibilities relating to the collection of information.

169

Your ideas for evidence

Description of evidence	Location of evidence	Opportunities for cross-referencing	Reflection and analysis

K&U links

Suggested reading for knowledge and understanding purposes:

Cole, G.A., *Management: Theory and Practice*, 5th edition, chapters 16, 17 and 19.

Needham, D. et al., *Business for Higher Awards,* chapter 9.

Cross-referencing

Evidence and knowledge from this element can be used in the following mandatory units of NVQ Management Level 3: **A1**, **B1**; and the following optional units: **C15**, **F7**.

Element **D1.1**   Gather required information

Performance Criterion

(b) *You take prompt and effective action to overcome problems in gathering relevant information.*

> You can link to the previous performance criterion in this element, if appropriate and relevant. Explain any specific problems that you have experienced when obtaining the information required. Detail your actions when dealing with the problems.

Interpretation

- What kinds of problems have you experienced?
- What action did you take to overcome them?
- What was the outcome?

Candidate illustration

Event route
Graham detailed problems concerning accuracy of the weekly bed occupancy information (see PC (a)). Since the unit offered respite care services, residents could move in and out of the unit within a week, making occupancy information inaccurate. To overcome this, Graham developed an interim mid-week occupancy check. The results were forwarded to the central office if there was a deviation from planned occupancy levels. In this way, unplanned under- or over-occupancy levels were monitored. Examples of the information collected during the interim check were submitted as evidence. Graham also obtained a witness testimony from his line manager confirming his actions and stating that Graham had obtained authorisation to implement the new system. Graham clearly explained his actions in his analysis of the evidence.

Event route
Emma explained an incident where, while gathering information for the ISO 9000 working party (see PC (a)), she had been unable to locate anything relating to implementation of ISO 9000 in her field, electronics production. To overcome the problem, she contacted the Institute of Management (to which she was affiliated), who assisted her in obtaining references from CD-ROM and Internet sources, giving Emma a broader research base. Emma detailed the incident in a personal statement and submitted examples of printed Internet and CD-ROM information as evidence.

Ideas for evidence

- Details of the problems.
- Examples of information gathered following the resolution of problems.
- Personal report detailing the problem and your actions.
- Witness testimony from others involved confirming your actions.

Your ideas for evidence

Description of evidence	Location of evidence	Opportunities for cross-referencing	Reflection and analysis

K&U links

Suggested reading for knowledge and understanding purposes:

Cole, G.A., *Management: Theory and Practice*, 5th edition, chapters 16, 17 and 19.

Needham, D. et al., *Business for Higher Awards*, chapter 9.

Cross-referencing

Evidence and knowledge from this element can be used in the following mandatory units of NVQ Management Level 3: **A1**, **B1**; and the following optional units: **C15**, **F7**.

Element D1.1   Gather required information

Performance Criterion

(c) *You record and store the information that you gather according to your organisation's systems and procedures.*

> You could link to the previous performance criteria in this element, if appropriate and relevant. Detail any organisational requirements that inform your methods of recording and storing information. Explain how you have recorded and stored specific items of information in line with these systems and procedures. Systems and procedures may be formal or informal throughout this element.

Interpretation

- How do you record and store information?
- Which formal or informal organisational requirements inform your methods of recording and storing information?

Candidate illustration

Event route
Graham cross-referenced to the completed bed occupancy pro-forma used in PC (a) of this element. He explained its uses in his analysis.

Event route
Emma explained how the information regarding ISO 9000 was stored and indexed using a lever arch file. The file was photographed and the picture used as evidence. Emma invited her NVQ assessor to visit her workplace to observe the file. She also submitted a personal report explaining the uses of the file.

Ideas for evidence

- Cross-reference to existing evidence used in this element, if relevant.
- Examples of pro-formas and standardised storage and recording methods.
- Personal statement explaining your storage and recording of information.
- Observational assessment from your NVQ assessor.

Your ideas for evidence

Description of evidence	Location of evidence	Opportunities for cross-referencing	Reflection and analysis

K&U links

Suggested reading for knowledge and understanding purposes:

Cole, G.A., *Management: Theory and Practice*, 5th edition, chapters 16, 17 and 19.

Needham, D. et al., *Business for Higher Awards*, chapters 9 and 25.

Cross-referencing

Evidence and knowledge from this element can be used in the following mandatory units of NVQ Management Level 3: **A1, B1**; and the following optional units: **C15, F7**.

Element D1.1 Gather required information

Performance Criterion

(d) The information that you gather is accessible in the required format to authorised people only.

You can link to previous performance criteria in this element, if appropriate and relevant. Detail specific items of information. Explain how you made that information available to others. Highlight any issues concerning confidentiality and access to information.

Interpretation

▮ How is information made available to others?

▮ Are there specific formats appropriate for certain kinds of information?

▮ How is authorisation given to people to allow them to access information?

Candidate illustration

Event route
Graham cross-referenced to the completed bed occupancy pro-forma evidenced in PC (a) of this element. In addition, he wrote a personal statement explaining the standardised format and its routine completion and supply to a specific person in the central office.

Event route
Emma cross-referenced to the evidence submitted for PC (c) of the element. She also submitted the minutes of an ISO 9000 meeting, where the lever arch file was identified as the most appropriate system for indexing and storing the information. Emma explained in her analysis that the file was available to steering group members and was not allowed to be removed from a central point.

Ideas for evidence

▮ Examples of formats:
   – pro-formas;
   – indexed reports and information.

▮ Explanations of formats.

▮ Witness testimony from others involved.

Your ideas for evidence

Description of evidence	Location of evidence	Opportunities for cross-referencing	Reflection and analysis

K&U links   Suggested reading for knowledge and understanding purposes:

Cole, G.A., *Management: Theory and Practice,* 5th edition, chapters 16, 17 and 19.

Needham, D. et al., *Business for Higher Awards,* chapters 9 and 25.

Cross-referencing   Evidence and knowledge from this element can be used in the following mandatory units of NVQ Management Level 3: **A1**, **B1**; and the following optional units: **C15**, **F7**.

Element D1.1   **Gather required information**

Performance Criterion

(e) You identify possible improvements to systems and procedures and pass these on to the appropriate people.

> To meet the requirements of this performance criterion you will need to detail specific instances where you have made recommendations for the improvement of systems and procedures for recording and storing information. Explain the circumstances and identify who the recommendations were made to.

Interpretation

■ What kinds of recommendations have you made?

■ Why were they made?

■ To whom were the recommendations made?

Candidate illustration

Event route
Graham cross-referenced to the evidence used in PC (b) of this element. He had detailed how an accuracy problem was overcome by creating an interim checking system for bed occupancy levels.

Event route
As some of the ISO 9000 documents and reports that Emma obtained were large and complex, she suggested the introduction of an indexing system to the rest of the group. Emma explained the system in her analysis and submitted photocopies of the indexing system as evidence. She also submitted a witness testimony obtained from the group leader confirming her actions.

Ideas for evidence

■ Cross-reference to existing evidence used in this element, if relevant.

■ Examples of suggestions for improvements that you have made.

■ Details of the suggestions once they have been put into action.

■ Witness testimony from others involved.

Your ideas for evidence

Description of evidence	Location of evidence	Opportunities for cross-referencing	Reflection and analysis

K&U links

Suggested reading for knowledge and understanding purposes:

Cole, G.A., *Management: Theory and Practice*, 5th edition, chapters 16, 17 and 19.

Needham, D. et al., *Business for Higher Awards*, chapter 9.

Cross-referencing

Evidence and knowledge from this element can be used in the following mandatory units of NVQ Management Level 3: **A1**, **B1**; and the following optional units: **C15**, **F7**.

Element D1.2 Inform and advise others

Performance Criterion

(a) *You give information and advice at a time and place, and in a form and manner, appropriate to the needs of recipients.*

> You must give specific examples of when you have informed and advised others. Explain the context and detail how the information was provided. Consider your knowledge of recipients and the nature of the information and advice given. Information and advice must be both spoken and written across this element.

Interpretation

■ When have you provided information to others?

■ How did you ensure that your methods of communication and timing were appropriate?

Candidate illustration

Event route
Throughout this element, Graham focused on the provision of information and advice to individual team members during supervision sessions. Graham explained that he set monthly supervision dates with each member of his team, and sessions were always held in the privacy of his office. As evidence he submitted a photocopied extract from his diary, detailing two planned supervision sessions with members of his team. He obtained a witness testimony from one of his team confirming his actions. Graham also submitted a completed supervision record, highlighting areas of information and advice offered to staff. To maintain confidentiality, the names of the staff members involved were deleted.

Event route
Emma linked to her evidence from Element D1.1 for most of this element. For this performance criterion, she cross-referenced to the evidence used in PC (a) of Element D1.1. The examples of information relating to ISO 9000 were highlighted by Emma to identify areas of relevance. Emma explained that the information was discussed by the ISO 9000 working party during meetings. Examples of minutes of a group meeting were also submitted, showing that Emma led a discussion on the ISO 9000 information.

Ideas for evidence

■ Schedules of meeting or supervision sessions.

■ Details of the information and advice given.

■ Witness testimony from others involved.

Your ideas for evidence

Description of evidence	Location of evidence	Opportunities for cross-referencing	Reflection and analysis

K&U links

Suggested reading for knowledge and understanding purposes:

Cole, G.A., *Management: Theory and Practice*, 5th edition, chapters 19 and 26.

Needham, D. et al., *Business for Higher Awards*, chapters 9 and 14.

Cross-referencing

Evidence and knowledge from this element can be used in the following mandatory units of NVQ Management Level 3: **A1**, **B1**, **C4**; and the following optional units: **C9**, **C12**, **E5**, **E8**, **F5**.

Inform and advise others

Performance Criterion

(b) The information you give is accurate, current, relevant and sufficient.

> You can link to the previous performance criterion in this element, if appropriate and relevant. Detail the nature of the information provided. Explain how you ensured it was appropriate information before providing it to others.

Interpretation

- What kinds of information have you given to others?
- How did you ensure that the information was appropriate before providing it?

Candidate illustration

Event route
Graham cross-referenced to the supervision documentation used in PC (a) of this element. The documentation showed advice given to a team member about the interpretation of new organisational procedures for lifting and handling residents. The supervision documentation also contained an action point, in which Graham had agreed to obtain the organisational policy document supporting lifting and handling procedures for the member of staff. Graham obtained a witness testimony from the staff member confirming that he had received the policy document from Graham.

Event route
Emma cross-referenced to the evidence used in PC (a) of Element D1.1. The evidence contained examples of information provided to the ISO 9000 working party, dated and referenced to show currency and reliability of sources. Emma also cross-referenced to the minutes of the group meeting (see PC (a) of this element), which showed that she had led a discussion on the information provided.

Ideas for evidence

- Cross-reference to evidence used in this element, if relevant.
- Examples of information provided.
- Minutes of meetings where information has been discussed.
- Supervision notes.
- Witness testimony from recipients of the information confirming relevance and sufficiency.

Your ideas for evidence

Description of evidence	Location of evidence	Opportunities for cross-referencing	Reflection and analysis

K&U links

Suggested reading for knowledge and understanding purposes:

Cole, G.A., *Management: Theory and Practice,* 5th edition, chapters 19 and 26.

Needham, D. et al., *Business for Higher Awards,* chapter 9.

Cross-referencing

Evidence and knowledge from this element can be used in the following mandatory units of NVQ Management Level 3: **A1**, **B1**, **C4**; and the following optional units: **C9**, **C12**, **E5**, **E8**, **F5**.

Element D1.2 # Inform and advise others

Performance Criterion

(c) *The advice you give is consistent with your organisation's policy, procedures and resource constraints.*

> You should try to link to previous performance criteria in this element, if appropriate and relevant. Detail any organisational policies and procedures that have informed the content of the advice provided.

Interpretation

▌ Which organisational policies and procedures are relevant?

▌ How did these inform the advice that you gave?

Candidate illustration

Event route
Graham cross-referenced to PC (b) of this element. The evidence was a supervision document, noting an enquiry from the supervisee. He highlighted the notes of the discussion relating to interpretation of organisational policy and procedures on lifting and handling. In his analysis of evidence, Graham explained how his advice supported putting procedures into action in the workplace.

Event route
Emma evidenced a memo, sent to her by the production manager, initially requesting her participation in the ISO 9000 group. The memo also requested that Emma research ISO 9000 on behalf of the group and to supply relevant information for discussion. Emma also cross-referenced to evidence submitted for Element D1.1, PC (b), where she had obtained information from a variety of sources using CD-ROM and Internet technology. In her analysis, Emma explained that these services were used as they allowed the organisation access to information that would otherwise have been unavailable owing to resource constraints, which would have limited the scope of the advice that Emma could give.

Ideas for evidence

▌ Cross-reference to evidence used in this element, if relevant.

▌ Examples of advice given.

▌ Minutes of meetings.

▌ Supervision documentation.

▌ Personal statement explaining how your advice was both supportive of organisational requirements and within resource constraints.

▌ Witness testimony from others involved confirming your actions.

Your ideas for evidence

Description of evidence	Location of evidence	Opportunities for cross-referencing	Reflection and analysis

K&U links

Suggested reading for knowledge and understanding purposes:

Cole, G.A., *Management: Theory and Practice,* 5th edition, chapters 19 and 26.

Needham, D. et al., *Business for Higher Awards,* chapters 9, 10 and 11.

Cross-referencing

Evidence and knowledge from this element can be used in the following mandatory units of NVQ Management Level 3: **A1, B1, C4**; and the following optional units: **C9, C12, E5, E8, F5.**

Element D1.2 **Inform and advise others**

Performance Criterion

(d) *You use reasoned arguments and appropriate evidence to support your advice.*

> Try to link to previous performance criteria in this element, if appropriate. Use specific examples to show how you qualified and justified the advice given to others. Detail any questions you were asked and how you answered them. Include any additional information used in support of your advice.

Interpretation

▪ How have you justified your advice?

▪ How were issues, questions and queries dealt with?

Candidate illustration

Event route

Graham cross-referenced to the evidence used in PCs (b) and (c) of this element. In his analysis he explained that the advice he had given to a member of staff on implementing the policies and procedures for lifting and handling residents had been supported by supplying the policy and procedures themselves. A witness testimony from the member of staff confirming this was also submitted.

Event route

Emma submitted minutes of an initial ISO 9000 group meeting as evidence. She highlighted a lengthy section of the minutes where timescales for implementing the ISO 9000 standard were discussed. The minutes showed that the majority of the group agreed on a timescale that Emma felt to be too ambitious. She advised the group of this and they requested further information. Emma's actions, reflected in the minutes, were to consult the ISO 9000 information file (see PC (c) of Element D1.1). She extracted articles and information supporting her advice that the timescales needed to be extended and distributed the information at the next meeting. The minutes of this meeting were also submitted as evidence, together with the information used to support Emma's advice. She clearly explained her actions in her analysis.

Ideas for evidence

▪ Cross-reference to evidence used in this element, if appropriate.

▪ Details of the circumstances.

▪ Minutes of meetings.

▪ Supervision documents.

▪ Examples of information used to qualify your advice.

Your ideas for evidence

Description of evidence	Location of evidence	Opportunities for cross-referencing	Reflection and analysis

K&U links

Suggested reading for knowledge and understanding purposes:

Cole, G.A., *Management: Theory and Practice,* 5th edition, chapters 19 and 26.

Needham, D. et al., *Business for Higher Awards,* chapters 9 and 10.

Cross-referencing

Evidence and knowledge from this element can be used in the following mandatory units of NVQ Management Level 3: **A1**, **B1**, **C4**; and the following optional units: **C9**, **C12**, **E5**, **E8**, **F5**.

Inform and advise others

Performance Criterion

(e) *You check and confirm recipients' understanding of the information and advice you have given them.*

> Again, link to previous performance criteria in this element, if appropriate. Following the provision of information and advice, explain how you have confirmed recipients' understanding. Recipients should include at least two of the following across this element: team members, peers, higher-level managers, or sponsors and external people.

Interpretation

▐ When have you needed to ensure others' understanding of information and advice that you have provided?

▐ Why was this necessary?

▐ How did you confirm understanding?

Candidate illustration

Event route
Graham continued to focus on the information given to a member of staff regarding changes to lifting and handling procedures (see PCs (a), (b), (c) and (d) of this element). Following the provision of the information, Graham agreed to review the implementation of the procedures with the member of staff at subsequent supervision sessions. Graham submitted a copy of the notes made during the next supervision session, highlighting the member of staff's performance when lifting and handling. The notes also recorded a discussion in which Graham had asked the member of staff to explain the procedures and his approach to carrying them out. In his analysis, Graham explained that he asked questions to check the member of staff's understanding of the procedures. This met part of the requirements of this PC, but Graham's assessor asked him to provide evidence involving another recipient (in line with the PC.)

Event route
Emma cross-referenced to the minutes of the ISO 9000 steering group meeting (see PC (a) of this element). When leading the discussion on ISO 9000 information, Emma had proposed a question and answer session to enable other members of the group to seek more information and clarify issues. Emma explained her actions in her analysis and highlighted the relevant parts of the minutes. As Emma's ISO 9000 group comprised peers and higher-level managers, she did not have to submit any additional evidence.

Ideas for evidence
- Cross-reference to evidence used in this element, if appropriate.
- Supervision documentation.
- Minutes of meetings.
- Details of question and answer sessions you have run.

Your ideas for evidence

Description of evidence	Location of evidence	Opportunities for cross-referencing	Reflection and analysis

K&U links

Suggested reading for knowledge and understanding purposes:

Cole, G.A., *Management: Theory and Practice*, 5th edition, chapters 19 and 26.

Needham, D. et al., *Business for Higher Awards*, chapters 10 and 14.

Cross-referencing

Evidence and knowledge from this element can be used in the following mandatory units of NVQ Management Level 3: **A1, B1, C4**; and the following optional units: **C9, C12, E5, E8, F5**.

Element D1.2 Inform and advise others

Performance Criterion

(f) You maintain confidentiality according to your organisation's requirements.

Once again, link to previous performance criteria in this element, if appropriate and relevant. Explain your organisation's requirements regarding confidentiality of information. Give a specific example of when you have complied with these requirements in informing and advising others.

Interpretation

- What are your organisation's requirements regarding confidentiality of information?
- How have you complied with these when providing information and advice to others?
- What were the circumstances?

Candidate illustration

Event route
Graham cross-referenced to the evidence used in PC (a) of this element, where he explained and evidenced the environment used for supervision sessions. The evidence also included a witness testimony from a member of Graham's staff confirming that confidentiality was maintained throughout the supervision process.

Event route
Emma detailed her filing system for the storage of staff's personal files and confidential information. In her analysis, she explained that all files were kept locked in her office and that she kept the key herself to restrict access to personal information. Emma took a photograph of the cabinet as evidence and invited her NVQ assessor to her workplace to observe it and its contents.

Ideas for evidence

- Cross-reference to evidence used in this element, if appropriate and relevant.
- Details of confidential environments used to provide sensitive information and advice.
- Photographic evidence.
- Observational assessment by your NVQ assessor.
- Witness testimony from others involved.

Your ideas for evidence

Description of evidence	Location of evidence	Opportunities for cross-referencing	Reflection and analysis

K&U links   Suggested reading for knowledge and understanding purposes:

Cole, G.A., *Management: Theory and Practice,* 5th edition, chapters 19 and 26.

Needham, D. et al., *Business for Higher Awards,* chapters 24 and 25.

Cross-referencing   Evidence and knowledge from this element can be used in the following mandatory units of NVQ Management Level 3: **A1, B1, C4**; and the following optional units: **C9, C12, E5, E8, F5**.

Element D1.2 **Inform and advise others**

Performance Criterion

(g) *You seek feedback from recipients about the information and advice you provide, and use this feedback to improve the ways in which you give information and advice.*

> You will need to detail specific circumstances where you have sought this kind of feedback from others. Explain the feedback and its impact on your approach to giving information and advice.

Interpretation

▪ How have you sought feedback from recipients about the information and advice you have given them?

▪ What was the nature of that feedback?

▪ How did you use the feedback to confirm or improve your methods of providing information and advice?

Candidate illustration

Event route
Graham was reviewing the notice board system that he used in the workplace to communicate general memos from the central office. He raised the review in a team meeting and requested feedback on the system from members of staff. The feedback showed that not everyone remembered to read the board regularly and that it was not possible to tell who had read what before notices were removed. Graham used the feedback to create a sheet for people to initial to show they had read important information. The minutes of the meeting and an example of a partially completed sheet were used as evidence. Graham clearly explained the evidence and his actions in his analysis.

Event route
At an ISO 9000 meeting, Emma requested feedback on the information file and indexing system (see PC (c) of Element D1.1). She requested specific detail on the file's ease of use and the relevance of the content. Emma made notes of the number of remarks made and used the feedback to further develop the file, adding colour codes to help people quickly identify sections of interest. The notes made, and a witness testimony from a member of the steering group confirming Emma's actions, were submitted as evidence.

Ideas for evidence

▪ Cross-reference to evidence used in this element, if appropriate and relevant.

▪ Details of feedback received:
   – minutes of meetings;
   – notes made;
   – emails;
   – memos;
   – correspondence.

■ Details of actions taken in response to feedback:
  – examples of changes made.

■ Witness testimony from others involved confirming your actions.

Your ideas for evidence

Description of evidence	Location of evidence	Opportunities for cross-referencing	Reflection and analysis

K&U links

Suggested reading for knowledge and understanding purposes:

Cole, G.A., *Management: Theory and Practice,* 5th edition, chapters 19 and 26.

Needham, D. et al., *Business for Higher Awards,* chapters 10 and 14.

Cross-referencing

Evidence and knowledge from this element can be used in the following mandatory units of NVQ Management Level 3: **A1, B1, C4**; and the following optional units: **C9, C12, E5, E8, F5**.

Element **D1.3**   Hold meetings

Performance Criterion

(a) *You give sufficient notice of the meeting to allow the necessary people to attend.*

> Make sure you focus on specific occasions where you have set dates for meetings. Detail how notice was given. Explain, given the purpose of the meeting and the responsibilities of the people attending, the significance of the amount of notice provided. Meetings should involve the following people across this element: those within your organisation and external people.

Interpretation

- When have you called meetings?
- What was their purpose?
- Who was required to attend?
- How did this impact on the amount of notice given?

Candidate illustration

Event route

Graham focused on the routine monthly team meetings that he chaired. He explained in his analysis that he set a schedule in December for meetings over the coming year and distributed it to members of his team. The schedule was submitted as evidence. Graham also wrote a personal statement detailing the timing of the meetings in relation to shift patterns to ensure that all staff could attend at least half of the meetings throughout the year without disrupting the workplace. (See Appendix 1.)

Event route

Emma focused on a specific meeting she had called with staff following the decision to implement the additional night shift in the factory (see Unit A1, Element A1.3, PC (a)). She distributed the agenda for the meeting to all her staff and her manager, together with a memo containing timescale instructions three weeks prior to the date of the meeting. The memo requested recipients to add items to the agenda for discussion at the meeting. Emma included the original agenda and memo as evidence and explained her actions in her analysis.

Ideas for evidence

- Details of notice given:
  – agendas;
  – memos;
  – schedules for routine meetings.

- Personal statement explaining your actions.

Your ideas for evidence

Description of evidence	Location of evidence	Opportunities for cross-referencing	Reflection and analysis

K&U links

Suggested reading for knowledge and understanding purposes:

Cole, G.A., *Management: Theory and Practice,* 5th edition, chapters 7, 8 and 26.

Needham, D. et al., *Business for Higher Awards,* chapter 10.

Cross-referencing

Evidence and knowledge from this element can be used in the following mandatory units of NVQ Management Level 3: **A1, B1, C1, C4**; and the following optional units: **C9, C12, E5, E8**.

Hold meetings

**Performance
Criterion**

(b) *You make clear the purpose and objectives of the meeting at the start.*

> You must provide details about specific meetings. Highlight when the purpose and objectives were communicated to those attending, and explain how they were communicated. The purpose of the meetings must cover one of the following across the element: information giving, consultation and decision making.

Interpretation

▉ When are the purpose and objectives of meetings communicated?

▉ How are they communicated?

**Candidate
illustration**

Event route
Both Graham and Emma cross-referenced to the evidence used for PC (a) of this element, highlighting their evidence to show where purposes and objectives were stated. (See Appendix 1.)

Ideas for evidence

▉ Cross-reference to evidence used in this element, if appropriate and relevant.

▉ Details of purposes and objectives of meetings:
  – agendas;
  – memos;
  – schedules detailing meetings.

▉ Emails sent.

▉ Correspondence.

▉ Items from notice boards.

Your ideas for evidence

Description of evidence	Location of evidence	Opportunities for cross-referencing	Reflection and analysis

K&U links

Suggested reading for knowledge and understanding purposes:

Cole, G.A., *Management: Theory and Practice,* 5th edition, chapters 7, 8 and 26.

Needham, D. et al., *Business for Higher Awards,* chapters 10 and 11.

Cross-referencing

Evidence and knowledge from this element can be used in the following mandatory units of NVQ Management Level 3: **A1**, **B1**, **C1**, **C4**; and the following optional units: **C9**, **C12**, **E5**, **E8**.

Element D1.3 Hold meetings

Performance Criterion

(c) *Your style of leadership helps people to make useful contributions.*

> You will need to explain your approach to chairing or leading meetings. Detail instances where you have assisted, requested or encouraged others to make useful contributions during the meeting.

Interpretation

- What is your approach to chairing or leading meetings?
- How do you encourage others to contribute during meetings?
- Why is this important?

Candidate illustration

Event route

Graham submitted two examples of the minutes of team meetings as evidence for this PC. He highlighted specific items from the minutes showing that he had requested ideas, feedback and issues for discussion from members of the team relating to agenda items. He also clearly explained his approach in a personal statement (see Appendix 1). However, Graham's assessor felt that his use of a personal statement was, in this instance, insufficient. She recommended that Graham support his claims through the use of a witness testimony.

Event route

In her analysis, Emma explained her approach to chairing the night shift implementation meeting (see PC (a) of this element). She included the original agenda she had distributed, together with the final agenda containing additional items from the team and her manager. She also submitted the minutes of the meeting, which recorded discussion of the items on the agenda and the resulting action points that were agreed.

Ideas for evidence

- Cross-reference to evidence used in this element, if appropriate and relevant.
- Witness testimony confirming your approach from people who attended the meeting.
- Agendas of meetings.
- Minutes of meetings.

Your ideas for evidence

Description of evidence	Location of evidence	Opportunities for cross-referencing	Reflection and analysis

K&U links Suggested reading for knowledge and understanding purposes:

Cole, G.A., *Management: Theory and Practice*, 5th edition, chapters 7, 8 and 26.

Mullins, L.J., *Management and Organisational Behaviour*, 4th edition, chapter 8.

Needham, D. et al., *Business for Higher Awards*, chapters 10 and 11.

Cross-referencing Evidence and knowledge from this element can be used in the following mandatory units of NVQ Management Level 3: **A1**, **B1**, **C1**, **C4**; and the following optional units: **C9**, **C12**, **E5**, **E8**.

Element D1.3 Hold meetings

Performance Criterion

(d) You discourage unhelpful arguments and digressions.

> You can link to previous performance criteria in this element, if relevant. Detail meetings where digressions have occurred. Explain the reasons behind the digressions and show how you managed the situation to retain the focus of the meeting.

Interpretation

◼ When have arguments and digressions occurred?

◼ What was their nature?

◼ How did you deal with the situation?

Candidate illustration

Event route
Graham invited his NVQ assessor to observe him chairing a team meeting. Using a standardised pro-forma based on the competencies contained in the element, the assessor made notes on Graham's performance throughout the meeting. The completed pro-forma detailed the way Graham handled a digression from one of the key agenda points and was submitted as evidence.

Event route
In a personal statement, Emma detailed an argument that occurred during the night shift implementation meeting (see PC (a) of this element). The argument concerned shift patterns and involved members of the team who were prepared or unprepared to work the new shift. Emma took advice from all those involved and compiled a list of staff willing to be part of the new shift. The number exceeded the number required for the shift. Emma explained that the shift was attractive because of increased pay for night shift duty. Using the list, a rota for the night shift was agreed, allowing staff to join the shift on a rolling basis. The minutes of the meeting were cross-referenced from PC (c) of this element, and the agreed action points were clearly highlighted.

Ideas for evidence

◼ Cross-reference to existing evidence used in this element, if appropriate and relevant.

◼ Personal statement explaining the circumstances and your actions.

◼ Witness testimony confirming your actions from people who attended the meeting.

◼ Minutes of meetings.

◼ Records of observational assessment from your NVQ assessor.

Your ideas for evidence

Description of evidence	Location of evidence	Opportunities for cross-referencing	Reflection and analysis

K&U links Suggested reading for knowledge and understanding purposes:

Cole, G.A., *Management: Theory and Practice,* 5th edition, chapters 7, 8 and 26.

Needham, D. et al., *Business for Higher Awards,* chapters 10 and 14.

Cross-referencing Evidence and knowledge from this element can be used in the following mandatory units of NVQ Management Level 3: **A1, B1, C1, C4**; and the following optional units: **C9, C12, E5, E8.**

Element D1.3   Hold meetings

Performance Criterion

(e) The meeting achieves its objectives within the allocated time.

> Make sure you detail the purpose of the meeting you are focusing on. Explain how objectives were achieved and the significance of the timescales involved.

Interpretation

- What was the purpose of the meetings?
- Were objectives met?
- How was this achieved?
- What were the timescales involved?

Candidate illustration

Event route

Both Graham and Emma cross-referenced to the agendas and minutes of their meetings (see PCs (a) and (b) of this element). Agreed action points were highlighted in the minutes, and Emma and Graham linked these to the stated objectives in their analyses of evidence to show that the objectives were achieved. The duration of meetings was also highlighted in the minutes.

Ideas for evidence

- Agendas of meetings showing objectives.
- Minutes of meetings detailing outcomes to demonstrate the achievement of objectives.

Your ideas for evidence

Description of evidence	Location of evidence	Opportunities for cross-referencing	Reflection and analysis

K&U links

Suggested reading for knowledge and understanding purposes:

Cole, G.A., *Management: Theory and Practice,* 5th edition, chapters 7, 8 and 26.

Needham, D. et al., *Business for Higher Awards,* chapters 10 and 11.

Cross-referencing

Evidence and knowledge from this element can be used in the following mandatory units of NVQ Management Level 3: **A1, B1, C1, C4**; and the following optional units: **C9, C12, E5, E8**.

Element D1.3   Hold meetings

Performance Criterion

(f)   You give clear, accurate and concise information about the outcomes of the meeting promptly to those who need it.

> You will need to explain how you provide information on the outcomes of meetings to others. Detail who these people were and the timescales involved.

Interpretation

- How was information regarding the outcomes of meetings provided to others?
- To whom was the information provided?
- Why did these people require the information?
- What were the timescales involved?
- Why were the timescales appropriate?

Candidate illustration

Event route
In his analysis of evidence Graham explained that, when staff were unable to attend meetings, he made sure they received the minutes to keep them up to date with team and organisational developments. He obtained a witness testimony from a member of staff confirming his actions and included the memo sent with the minutes to members of staff who had missed meetings.

Event route
Emma routinely circulated minutes of meetings to her line manager and colleagues who led other staff teams. She cross-referenced to the minutes of the night shift implementation meeting (see PC (c) of this element) and submitted the minutes circulation list as evidence. Emma highlighted the date of circulation to show that it was close to the time of the meeting.

Ideas for evidence

- Cross-reference to evidence used in this element, if appropriate.
- Witness testimony from those involved.
- Personal statement explaining your actions.
- Examples of information provided:
  – minutes of meetings;
  – memos.
- Examples of minutes circulation lists.

Your ideas for evidence

Description of evidence	Location of evidence	Opportunities for cross-referencing	Reflection and analysis

K&U links

Suggested reading for knowledge and understanding purposes:

Cole, G.A., *Management: Theory and Practice,* 5th edition, chapters 7, 8 and 26.

Needham, D. et al., *Business for Higher Awards,* chapters 10 and 14.

Cross-referencing

Evidence and knowledge from this element can be used in the following mandatory units of NVQ Management Level 3: **A1, B1, C1, C4**; and the following optional units: **C9, C12, E5, E8**.

Glossary

Accredited Prior Learning/Achievement (APL/A) The formal recognition of your existing achievement, knowledge and/or skills.

Advice Formal support given to you by your advisor to help you achieve your NVQ.

Advisor The person allocated to help you achieve the requirements of the NVQ.

Assessment The process undertaken by the assessor of comparing the evidence you put forward with the NVQ standards in order to determine whether you are competent in that area.

Assessment centre The organisation responsible for the process of assessment, including quality assurance and the appointment and management of suitable assessors. These have to be approved by the awarding body.

Assessment decisions The formal decision made by your assessor. These take three forms: competent, not yet competent and insufficient evidence.

Assessors The people appointed by the assessment centre to judge your evidence against the NVQ standards.

Awarding body A body recognised by the lead body and responsible for 'packaging' NVQ standards into qualifications that can be awarded to candidates. There are currently 16 awarding bodies for the NVQ in Management at Level 3.

Candidate An individual who has registered with an awarding body and who has begun to develop a portfolio of evidence (i.e. you!).

Candidate questioning The process of generating evidence whereby the assessor or advisor will ask you questions and make a formal record of the process.

Competence The ability to perform your job to the nationally recognised standard.

Competent An assessment decision which confirms that your evidence meets the nationally recognised standards.

Elements of competence The description of a specific aspect of performance associated with a particular work activity.

Evidence Anything which is put forward in order to show competence within the NVQ framework.

Evidence collection The process of gathering evidence to put forward for assessment.

External verification Part of the quality assurance process, undertaken by the awarding body, which ensures that the assessment of candidates meets its requirements.

Insufficient evidence An assessment decision which means that you could not be assessed 'competent' because of a lack of evidence.

Internal verification Part of the quality assurance process, undertaken by the assessment centre, which ensures that the assessment process meets the standards of the awarding body.

Knowledge and understanding (K&U) The theoretical and underpinning knowledge relevant to your job.

Lead body An organisation responsible for identifying the nationally acceptable standards of performance relevant to a particular industry. The lead body for the Management NVQs is the Management Charter Initiative (MCI).

Level This reflects the amount of competence, knowledge, initiative, responsibility and autonomy associated with each stage in the NVQ framework. There are five levels of NVQ.

Management Charter Initiative (MCI) The lead body for the Management NVQs. Through consultation they have developed the management standards and are responsible for their upkeep.

Mandatory units The core or mandatory units of the NVQ reflect those activities that would normally be undertaken by all managers at a specific level of management. There are five mandatory units in the Management NVQ at Level 3.

National Council for Vocational Qualifications (NCVQ) Please see Qualifications and Curriculum Authority (QCA).

National Vocational Qualifications (NVQs) These are qualifications based on nationally recognised occupational standards which prescribe the expected standard of performance in a job.

Naturally occurring evidence This is evidence that occurs as a result of an activity in which you are already involved or will be undertaking as part of your normal working routine (usually termed 'performance evidence').

Not yet competent The assessment decision given when you have not proved your competence.

Observation The method of assessing evidence which relies on you demonstrating your competence in front of the assessor.

Observational analysis sheet A written record of the assessment process when it has been undertaken through observation.

Optional units The optional units of the NVQ allow you to select those that most closely reflect your areas of management responsibility. You should select two optional units from a choice of eight in the Management NVQ at Level 3.

Performance criterion (PC) The specific behaviour or outcome associated with an element of competence. These are the standards against which you are assessed.

Performance evidence Evidence that has occurred naturally as a result of your job (sometimes termed 'naturally occurring evidence').

Personal statements Accounts by candidates detailing work performance. They are often needed in order to contextualise performance evidence, i.e. to provide the assessor with some background or other necessary additional information or explanation.

Portfolio Your compilation of evidence used to demonstrate competence.

Qualifications and Curriculum Authority (QCA) The organisation responsible for overseeing all NVQs in the UK outside Scotland. It was formed in 1997, bringing together the National Council for Vocational Qualifications (NCVQ) and the School Curriculum and Assessment Authority (SCAA). The QCA formally recognises NVQs and audits the activity of awarding bodies.

Random sampling The process of choosing a sample of portfolios to be verified for quality assurance purposes.

Reflection and analysis The process of explanation you undertake to clarify why the evidence put forward meets the standards of competence stipulated by the NVQ.

Registration The process of signing up with an awarding body.

Scottish Qualifications Authority (SQA) The organisation responsible for overseeing all NVQs in Scotland. The SCA formally recognises SVQs and audits the activity of awarding bodies.

Scottish Vocational Qualification (SVQ) The Scottish equivalent of National Vocational Qualifications (NVQs).

Simulated training activities Any training or development opportunity outside the candidate's normal job which is undertaken purely to meet the requirements of the NVQ.

Standards The lead body's description of competence for a specific job.

Supplementary evidence Evidence that is put forward in addition to performance evidence. This is often in the form of personal statements or testimonies.

Units of competence A group of standards that reflect a specific area of a job.

Vocational education and training Education and training based on candidates' performance in their job, not in the classroom. Vocational qualifications 'focus on your performance at work, how you use your skills, apply your knowledge and the available resources to achieve results' (MCI, 1997).

Witness testimonies Statements made by others as to your performance in the workplace.

Bibliography

Beaumont, G., 1997, *Review of 100 NVQs and SVQs*, A Report Submitted to the Department for Education and Employment.

Cole, G.A., 1996, *Management: Theory and Practice*, 5th edition, Letts Educational, London.

Confederation of British Industry, 1987, *The Handy Report*.

Constable and McCormick, 1987, *The Making of British Managers*, BIM/CBI.

Dakers, H., 1996, *NVQs and How to Get Them*, Kogan Page.

Department for Education and Employment, 1996, 'The Specification of Knowledge and Understanding for NVQs and SVQs: Six Case Studies', *Competence and Assessment Briefing Series*, 11.

Department for Education and Employment, 1998, '*The Learning Age – A Renaissance for a New Britain*', Green Paper presented to Parliament by the Secretary of State for Education and Employment, HMSO.

Fletcher, S., 1992, *Competence-Based Assessment Techniques*, Kogan Page.

Handy, C., Gordon, C., Gow, I., Moloney, M. and Randlesome, C., 1987, *The Making of Managers*, NDEC/MSC/BIM.

Jessup, G., 1991, *Outcomes: NVQs and the Emerging Model of Education and Training*, Falmer Press.

Longworth, N. and Davies, W.K., 1996, *Lifelong Learning*, Kogan Page.

Management Charter Initiative (MCI), 1997, *What are Management Qualifications? An Introduction*.

Mullins, L.J., 1996, *Management and Organisational Behaviour*, 4th edition, Pitman Publishing, London.

Needham, D., Dransfield, R., Harris, R. and Coles, M., 1995, *Business for Higher Awards*, Heinemann, Oxford.

Qualifications and Curriculum Authority, 1997, *DataNews*, Issue 6, Winter.

Example of completed reflection and analysis documentation

ANALYSIS OF EVIDENCE.

Name: *Graham XXX*

NVQ LEVEL 3/4 – SUPERVISORY MANAGEMENT/MANAGEMENT STANDARDS.

(delete as applicable)

EL.	PERF. CRIT.	ANALYSIS and REFLECTION	EVID. REF.	AGREED (ASS'OR)
D1.3	(a)	I have included a copy of my monthly team meeting schedule (EV1). I set a schedule for the next 12 months' meetings in December each year and this schedule is then emailed to all relevant staff. I have also included a personal statement (EV2) which explains how I choose the timing of the meetings in relation to shift patterns to ensure that all staff could attend at least half of the meetings throughout the year without disrupting the workplace.	EV1 and EV2	
D1.3	(b)	Please see EV1 – this meeting schedule details routine agenda items, to be discussed during our monthly team meetings. In addition, about a fortnight before each meeting, a request goes out to staff for any additional agenda items (EV3). The final agenda is circulated at the beginning of each meeting (EV4).	EV3 and EV4	
D1.3	(c)	I have submitted two examples of the minutes of team meetings as evidence for this performance criterion (EV5 and EV6). I have highlighted specific items from the minutes that show how I request ideas, feedback and issues for discussion from members of the team relating to agenda items. In my personal statement (EV7), I have explained how my leadership style is conducive to receiving feedback and suggestions from my team members.	EV5 EV6 and EV7	

Please use additional sheets as required.

Example of completed assessor's feedback sheet

Assessor Feedback Sheet   Unit Number D1   Element 3

                                 NVQ Level ~~2~~ 3 ~~4 5~~

Name of Candidate Graham XXX   Name of Assessor Cathy Parker

Period of Evidence   From: September 1997   To: January 1998

Type of Evidence (tick as appropriate)

WORK BASED		TRAINING		OTHER	
Own original work	√	Project		Voluntary work	
Product of work	√	Assignment			
Personal report	√	Exercise(s)			
Diary/Logbook		Case-study			
Witness Testimony		Simulation			

Direct observation: Yes ☐   No ☑

Oral questioning necessary: Yes ☐   No ☑

Feedback

PC	Feedback	Summary of action to be taken	Assessment decision Competent Insufficient evidence Not yet competent
(a)	Your meeting schedule and personal statement clearly meet the requirements of this PC.	None	Competent
(b)	Your evidence displays competence.	None	Competent
(c)	Your use of a personal statement is not very suitable here. Please get at least one witness testimony which supports your claims.	At least one witness testimony to be submitted as additional evidence.	Insufficient evidence

Feedback continued overleaf: Yes ☐   No ☐

Assessment Decision

This candidate is ~~competent~~/not yet competent in this element.

Assessor's signature: Cathy Parker   Date: 13th March 1998

Index